CHESHIRE
THE SECRET WAR
1939-1945

CHESHIRE

THE SECRET WAR

1939–1945

Ron Freethy

COUNTRYSIDE BOOKS
NEWBURY BERKSHIRE

First published 2012
© Ron Freethy 2012

COUNTRYSIDE BOOKS
3 Catherine Road
Newbury, Berkshire

To view our complete range of books,
please visit us at
www.countrysidebooks.co.uk

ISBN 978 1 84674 294 1

Designed by Peter Davies, Nautilus Design
Produced through MRM Associates Ltd., Reading
Typeset by CJWT Solutions, St Helens
Printed by Berforts Information Press, Oxford

Contents

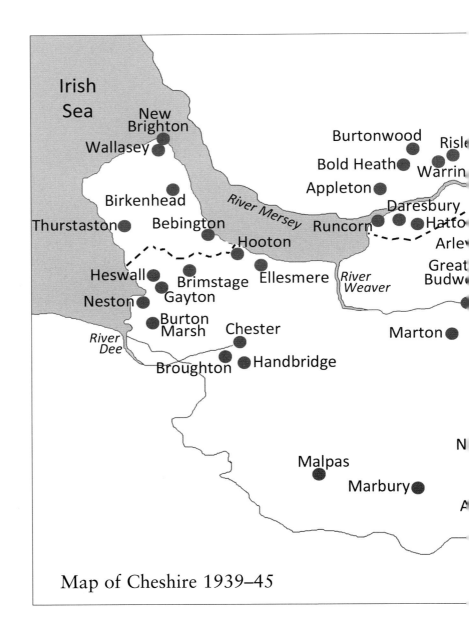

Map of Cheshire 1939–45

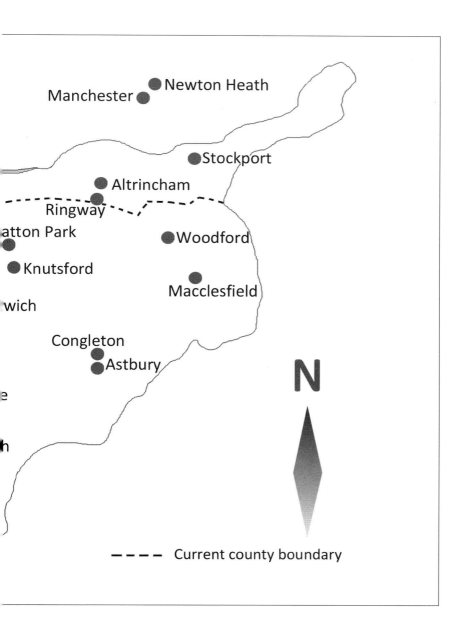

Manchester ● ● Newton Heath

● Stockport

● Altrincham

Ringway

atton Park ●

● Woodford

● Knutsford

● Macclesfield

wich

Congleton
●
● Astbury

e

h

N

- - - - Current county boundary

Introduction

This book sets out to record events experienced by those people of Cheshire who lived through the Second World War. It was a time when the residents of Cheshire learned to work hard and speak quietly. Careless talk, as the posters clearly pointed out, could cost lives.

The county boundary changes of 1974 have made it difficult, but thankfully not impossible, to record accurately Cheshire's role in the Second World War. The one-time Cheshire town of Stockport and its surrounding area is now officially a part of Greater Manchester, and the Wirral towns of Birkenhead and Wallasey are now in Merseyside. Both areas, however, were very much a part of Cheshire's war.

As I spoke to people around the county, it became obvious that a great deal of undercover work went on during the war, some of which is still cloaked in a blanket of secrecy. Alongside this vital work, however, men and women still had to carry on with their daily lives which changed dramatically when the war began in earnest. This is the story of those Cheshire folk and how they coped with the demands placed upon them both at work and at home.

There is no doubt that it is possible to misquote Winston Churchill and say that this wartime period was Britain's 'finest period' when the country was at its most resilient. It has on the whole been well-documented but biased in favour of long academic reports or large collections of images with short captions. What is in danger of being lost, however, are details of what was once secret and which some people are still reluctant to talk about today. Many of those who were there think that nobody is interested in what they did during the war years. Their memories, though, must not be lost and this is why this book has been written.

All writers who are compiling this sort of information are aware not so much of what they have discovered but what they have missed. All who read this book could do historians a great favour by collecting information about Cheshire and all other counties at war, thus ensuring that this source of history is not lost forever. I, myself, would be pleased to hear from any reader who has more material to add to the story of Cheshire's war.

Ron Freethy

Acknowledgements

I am grateful to all those who are featured in the text and also to some who are not specifically mentioned, such as curators of museums and reference libraries. I am also grateful to the police museums in both Manchester and Warrington. Harry Holmes, one-time public relations officer for AVRO and BAe Systems was, as ever, a flowing fountain of information. Harry is an eminent historian not only in the field of aviation but also with regard to submarine warfare and has always been generous with both his time and knowledge.

The staff at the publishers, Countryside Books, have been encouraging from start to finish and their editorial and production staff have, as always, been easy to work with.

This book, though, could never have been written without the support of my family. My wife Marlene has been chauffeur, typist, friendly critic and eagle-eyed proof reader. She has helped with this book despite health problems and so I am more grateful than usual. My grandson Thomas Toft has been present on vital research trips and has often taken some of the rough notes in places where 'two pens were better than one'.

Chapter 1

The Build-Up

Although victorious, the people of Britain were still reeling from the slaughter of the First World War when Hitler took over the bankrupt country of Germany in 1933. And when a massive influx of Germany tourists arrived in Britain, many in Britain did not see these people as a threat; after all they spent of lot of much needed money. Only a few realised that these tourists were actually very efficient spies. Hitler youth groups came on organised friendship tours of Britain, many travelling very slowly by bicycle and armed with the very best of cameras (at the time Germany led the world in the field of optics). They also brought with them German-published Baedeker guides which contained very accurate maps of Britain. Once here, they purchased Britain's own travel guides, such as the Shell books and the Ordnance Survey maps. Demand was such that many shops ran out of stock. It should be remembered that the Ordnance Survey maps were just that – they had been produced by the British Army at a time when there was a threat of a French invasion orchestrated by Napoleon. The Shell guides to the English counties were edited by John Betjeman who was recruited at the start of the Second World War to work in the Ministry of Information.

There is an argument which suggests that these maps and observations were used by the Germans as they planned the invasion of Britain – Operation *Sealion*, as it was code-named – and most agree with this view but obviously the Luftwaffe later photographed potential sites. Whilst the main invasion force would have been concentrated upon the south-east of England, there may well have been diversionary attacks perhaps in the north and launched from southern Ireland.

In the mid 1930s, German airships also toured Britain on what were described as 'goodwill visits', with more tourists armed with batteries of cameras. Another popular tourist network involved taking steamer trips around the coast. One of the vessels used was

As the Hindenburg airship flew over Barrow on a 'goodwill' mission, photographs were taken of the docks which proved useful to the Germans during the war. The airship also flew over Liverpool docks and the shipyards of Cammell Laird.

It is now known that the pleasure steamer SS Minden *which cruised around north-west England during the 1930s was a German spy ship.*

the SS *Minden* which was based out of Blackpool. What comes as something of a surprise is that the vessel was German-owned so naturally it was very popular with tourists from the Fatherland. The *Minden* toured the coast, including passing Liverpool and Birkenhead docks, and other areas that became potential targets once war began. And it wasn't just industrial sites that came under scrutiny. The Germans also paid great attention to cultural centres such as the historic cities of York, Bath and, indeed, Chester.

During the blitz of London, Coventry, Liverpool and Manchester in 1940 and 1941, however, the cultural towns and cities were not targeted. It was not until the devastating raid on the city of Lübek by Bomber Command in March 1942 that the Germans retaliated by attacking the city of Bath on 25th/26th April 1942 at the time of a full moon when 417 people were killed. Chester was put on high alert and the fire services and bomb dispersal teams in the area were prepared to move into Chester and the diversionary 'Starfish' sites (see chapter 3).

At the beginning of the war there were a few – but thankfully, only a few – British people who had Fascist leanings, some of them included prominent citizens in the north-west of England. I once met Rachael Kay-Shuttleworth at her home in Gawthorpe Hall, near Burnley who told me,

We all knew of aristocratic friends in Lancashire and Cheshire who had far right leanings and their identities will never ever be revealed. It would be difficult, however, to accuse them of outright treason because there is a vast difference between sympathy and planning direct action.

There is no doubt, however, that Sir Oswald Mosley and William Joyce, better known as Lord Haw Haw, had very firm North-West connections. The activities and views of Sir Oswald Mosley were quite transparent and his old family estate was at Trafford Park. It is somewhat ironic that during the conflict the Trafford Park Industrial Complex, close to the Manchester Ship Canal, contained a number of massive armaments factories.

Horace Parkinson has memories of his time in the war which covers many aspects of wartime industry,

I was a crewman in barges operating along the Ship canal and often passed alongside the Trafford Park factories. One of the skippers told me that he had a distant relative who worked as a maid when the Mosleys were in residence. I also remember passing through when the first AVRO Manchesters were on the assembly line. All my family worked for AVRO and we often met up at the Company Sports and Social Club near Macclesfield. During the war there were notices all over telling us to keep our work secret. I still have a copy of a photograph of the club taken in the 1920s showing workers relaxing. Six of my uncles worked at Woodford and all played football and cricket for the company. I was told that a bomber crew visited Woodford and a worker had said that he felt guilty playing football while the crews were risking their lives. 'Don't worry' he was told 'it is that sort of freedom that you are fighting for. Don't you think that fun can win battles?'

To the Germans, William Joyce was a 5 ft 6 ins 'giant'. He was a confused and not very pleasant individual however, and his propaganda broadcasts were seen by most British people as a comedy act. Born in 1906 and of Irish descent he joined the British Fascist party at the age of seventeen but it was not long before he was made very unwelcome because of his extreme views. He then joined the Conservative party but was very soon forced to resign. It has to be accepted that as war with Germany became inevitable the political divisions in Britain began to polarise. The very extreme right-wingers were in stark contrast to those on the left with firm Communist commitments. The industrial areas of the North-West were a flash point for the meeting of these opposing doctrines. Here was a breeding ground for agents supporting the views of Mosley and Joyce and the authorities began to secretly monitor the pair closely.

After an initial falling out, the infamous pair joined forces again and Joyce became the Minister of Propaganda under Mosley's leadership. However, the two soon fell out again and Joyce founded his own National Socialist Party which closely followed Hitler's blueprint. His manifesto laid out a plan for Germany taking over Britain, where there was to be no king or elected government. He made no secret of his dislike of the Jews, either.

After spreading his vitriolic views in Liverpool, Birkenhead and Stockport, he returned to his native Manchester where he was eventually arrested. I spoke at length to Duncan Broady, the Curator of the Manchester Police Museum, and Dennis Wood, a volunteer at the museum and a retired policeman. Dennis told me:

Every officer at that time was well aware of both Mosley and Joyce and the Cheshire force based in Warrington were also well informed.

*The AVRO Sports Club, near Macclesfield, seen here between the wars.
AVRO always had a real family atmosphere and encouraged youngsters
to join the company when they left school. (Horace Parkinson)*

Dennis showed me the cell in which William Joyce was confined. He was released in 1939, though one does wonder why, and then he surfaced in Berlin, from where he was soon spreading his messages over the air waves.

The activities of Mosley and Joyce were obviously well known but there was a feeling that there were spies under every bush and bed but how did you spot one? Everybody, especially those relaxing in the pubs, was encouraged to speak to strangers and quiz them about the local Rugby League Clubs and their history. Football, cricket and old films were subjects worthy of discussion, too. Car registration numbers were also something to look out for and the police and others, including teenagers, began collecting them. During the war there were fewer cars and other vehicles on the road and each town had its own unique combination of letters in front of the number so non-local cars were easily recognizable and could be checked out.

The spy mania which gripped Britain resulted in so-called 'foreign nationals' and camps were set up on the Isle of Man to house these largely innocent people. Ruth Gunter was one of them. She was twelve in 1940 and recalls these sad times,

My mother had worked in the silk mills of Macclesfield for more than twenty years and had paid her taxes and we owed nothing. Our father had actually fought for Britain in the First World War and worked all of his life until he died suddenly in 1938. Although we had a German name, our family had been in the area since 1876. Despite all this we were sent to a camp in the Isle of Man until the authorities came to their senses and sent us home. Our neighbours gave us a smashing party despite the rations and returned our cat which they had looked after for us. Our house had been spring-cleaned and there were flowers everywhere. Until the end of the war both me and my mum worked at the Ordnance factory at Hooton where we packed bullets which were fired at our enemy and neither of us could speak a word of German!

It would seem that the Manx people didn't like the way that some of the 'Nationals' were being treated and did their best to make these alien people feel wanted.

As the war continued, there were a few pleasant surprises as people who would not be expected to help turned their hands to the pump. One correspondent who lives near Chester and asked not to reveal her name told me,

> *One of my relatives could best be regarded as a career criminal but he was good at his job. He could open safes and was actually in prison when war was declared. He went to the Prison Governor asking if he could do something useful. He was given a very firm 'No' but three days later he was interviewed by a chap in a posh suit. He was soon set free and put to work looking after safes in which secret documents were stored for the use of the Invasion Committee. At first he was supervised but soon he was a trusted and respected worker. After the war he became a security officer and never looked back. He later told me that he won his own personal war thanks to the Germans.*

As plans to repel any assault were developed, Invasion Committees were set up all over Britain. It was assumed that there would be several attacks from the sea but this would be backed up by parachute landings. All possible landing sites were identified and on the Wirral and the Lancashire side of the Mersey, telegraph poles were planted on golf courses to resemble forests and strewn with barbed wire, whilst islands such as Hilbre in the Dee estuary were fortified. Not all these developments could be kept secret of course but plans as to how the resistance was to be co-ordinated were kept firmly under lock and key, with very limited access. Therefore, those with a knowledge of safes, both with regard to construction and their operation were in demand.

When the Germans overran France and the Dunkirk evacuation was stalled, the major problem had been the roads becoming blocked by civilian refugees. The Government feared the same thing happening here. Therefore, plans were put in place for all church bells to be rung in the event of a threatened invasion. Air Raid Wardens were to refer to the Air Raid Precautions Training Leaflet, which was also entitled *Advising the Public in the Event of Invasion*. The public were to 'stand firm' in order to leave the

In 1940, many people with foreign-sounding names like Ruth Gunter were rounded up as aliens and shepherded onto trains. They were then sent to the Isle of Man and placed in internment camps. However, it was soon realised that they were British people who posed no threat and most were released.

road and rail networks clear for the military. Joyce Middleton told me that her father was an Air Raid Warden in Birkenhead and he was not pleased to have to pay a penny for this confidential pamphlet. He also had to apply in writing to get his copy which he had to keep secure.

Actually this procedure made sense from a security point of view and there was also advice on how to immobilise motor vehicles and even bicycles so that they could not be used by any advancing force.

Another even more vital publication was entitled *Consolidated Instructions to Invasion Committees*. Again, copies of this were restricted and kept under lock and key until such time as an invasion was imminent. Some of the instructions contained in these pamphlets sound heartless to us in the present day but during war conditions they made great sense. Priorities were to be given to the military and the welfare of the people was of secondary importance. The army, including the Home Guard, police, fire service and the ARP wardens were to be controlled from a central point. In the case of the Wirral and Cheshire, the factories and the docks had either to be protected or, in an extreme situation, destroyed.

A network of defensive works was already in place, including the telegraph poles along places such as golf courses as already described. There were miles of barbed wire with much of this produced in the

<u>Confidential</u>

AIR RAID PRECAUTIONS
TRAINING PAMPHLET No. 3
(August, 1941)

ADVISING THE PUBLIC
IN THE EVENT OF
INVASION

(NOTES FOR THE GUIDANCE OF AIR RAID WARDENS)

Issued by the Ministry of Home Security

LONDON
HIS MAJESTY'S STATIONERY OFFICE
1941
Price 1d. net

**Copies will be sold only on written application to
H.M. Stationery Office, York House, Kingsway, W.C.2,
by a principal of a public utility company or industrial
or commercial concern**

Pamphlet No. 3 was familiar to all ARP wardens.

factories in and around Warrington and also huge blocks of concrete designed to stop or delay the movement of tanks. Pill boxes were built all over Cheshire and the rest of the country. They were not erected in a haphazard manner but each was specially designed in order to protect vulnerable places such as river crossings, bridges and possible landing points. They varied in shape but each box had slits from which machine guns could cover an advancing force.

Only a few of these pillboxes now remain and they are obvious even to an untrained eye. This was not the case though at the time. All the boxes were camouflaged and in the rural areas of Cheshire they were made to look like haystacks, with 'dummy sheep and cattle' grazing around them. Among the pillboxes still to be found in Cheshire is a fine example at the old Parkgate railway station which can be seen in the former station yard. No doubt it would have been camouflaged, perhaps to look like an old wagon. Another interesting box can be seen at Saltney which was a powerful strongpoint guarding a crossing point of the River Dee. There are other good examples at Hargrave and another opposite Manning Lane at Hoole.

These pillboxes were placed in defensive rings and, sadly, not all counties have recorded their positions. This is not the case with Cheshire, though, and I am grateful for the help I was given by the reference library in Chester.

What was absolutely vital was to keep all of these defensive systems in contact so communications were vital. The German planners also knew how critical this was and would soon have cut power lines. Retired post office engineers with a knowledge of Morse code were drawn into the net, along with Scout and Guide groups who knew semaphore. Those with bicycles or who could ride horses were particularly welcomed.

One aspect of the communications system which has not been fully documented was the pigeon post. This was pioneered in the industrial areas of the North-West, including Cheshire. To begin with, the Racing Pigeon Fanciers clubs were contacted and then a few men were singled out and asked to sign the Official Secrets

The pillbox still standing at the old Parkgate railway station.

Saltney pillbox, overlooking the River Dee.

Act. The best of the birds were provided with rations and could be sent to vulnerable points. From the 1900s onwards the railway companies had generated good profits by running pigeon specials. The birds were taken to release points and the pigeons then flew to their home roost. The first bird to arrive home was welcomed by its owner who received a substantial cash prize. This led to a trade in purpose-built wicker baskets and in sophisticated timing devices. There were also detailed plans in place to prevent cheating and this system could be easily adapted to a secret system. All that had to be done was to attach a message to the bird's leg and collect the message from a centrally controlled loft. Apart from the Germans, though, the homing pigeon had another enemy – the peregrine falcon. Ben Alston whose father had an allotment and pigeon loft very close to Burtonwood airbase told me that his father called the peregrines a 'mobile bloody slaughter house' because they swooped at high speeds on birds in flight, including pigeons. There was a plan to find where the peregrine nest sites were and the birds would have been shot on sight when the invasion looked likely.

Once the invasion was underway all the plans so far discussed were to be put into operation. There is no doubt that as the Germans gained a foothold the most prestigious houses would have been taken over by high-ranking officers. There was a system of well-trained teams who were in place as 'sleepers' around the large houses. They could disappear into holes in the ground and emerge to liquidate the German officers. In the early 1980s, I co-presented a series of programmes with the late Bob Smithies for Granada TV and we explored a number of mansions including Lyme Hall. Whilst we were looking for deer in the park, we found a depression in the ground which looked very like what was left of one of these hit squad hideouts. It is quite probable that most of these old hideouts will have been lost forever but there is no doubt that they existed and were well planned.

There were other groups who were trained to head for the hills of nearby North Wales and also to the Peak District reached from

Congleton. They were tough men who had worked in the gritstone quarries and the mines. They knew from a lifetime of experience just where hideouts could be protected from prying eyes and were well used to working in claustrophobic conditions.

Spies and the secret service have long been the subject of novels but as the war clouds hovered over Britain, this was not a novel but stark reality.

Chapter 2

Censorship, Civil Defence and the Blitz

The function of the Censor was twofold: firstly, information had to be denied to the enemy and secondly, the morale of the civilian population had to be maintained. The setting up of a Ministry of Information was discussed as early as 1935 but it was only officially initiated on the day that war was finally declared on 3rd September 1939. A prominent member in the early days was the poet John Betjeman (1906–1984) who was keen to point out that his ancestors were Dutch and not German. Another was the novelist Graham Greene (1904–1991) who later specialised in spy novels which is hardly surprising given his background.

The majority of the Ministry's members were recruited from the upper classes who, with their 'cut glass' accents, were often the subject of rather cruel humour although it could be said that it was good for morale to have someone to laugh at. Comedians coined the phrase 'The Ministry of Aggravation and Mysteries' and Liverpool-born comedian Tommy Handley used it to effect in his radio programme, *It's That Man Again* (ITMA).

Although the Ministry did not get off to a good start, things did improve from July 1941 when Winston Churchill brought in the efficient Brendan Bracken, with Sir Walter Monkton, to ensure that literally thousands of censorship orders were drawn up. By January 1941 the *Daily Worker* newspaper had been closed down and in March 1942 the *Daily Mirror* was threatened with closure.

A conscious decision was made at high level in government office to 'massage' (or should I say 'fiddle') the figures relating to both military and civilian casualties. During the Battle of Britain and also in the Blitz of Britain, figures were issued to produce the most optimistic statistics even though these were not accurate.

It is no wonder that there was an acute shortage of paper when it is realised just how many posters, books and manuals were published. Posters as numerous as autumn leaves appeared everywhere and kept billstickers hard at work. One which read '**Your** courage, **your** cheerfulness, **your** resolution will bring us Victory' sounds to me to be very condescending. Much more effective were the funny posters featuring Mrs Leaky Mouth, Miss Teacup Whisper, Mr Glum Pot and the one that said 'Be Like Dad, Keep Mum'.

There were also people employed as Censorship spies who were sent into factories, bombed out areas, pubs, cafés, cinemas and theatres. Unfortunately, most spoke 'posh' and were very subjective but they did pick up on the general mood. The Censor's job was made more difficult in the days before America entered the war as the figures were manipulated to appeal to the American public and to encourage them to side with Britain.

There were particular problems in the early days when the Battle of the Atlantic was not going well. It has to be admitted that the British Navy was both self-confident and under-prepared. The so-called British Secret Codes were far from secure as I was told in no uncertain manner when I spoke to Oxford graduate, Joyce Openshaw, who worked in the cipher office based at Derby

House in Liverpool. Joyce, in her 93rd year when I spoke with her in 2009 told me,

> *To begin with, our secret codes were a joke. Every vessel leaving the port had a code book and nobody knew for sure how many had been printed. On one of my few days off in late 1939 I took the ferry over the Mersey to meet some friends near to Perch Rock in New Brighton. A young naval officer arrived with his civilian girl friend in an open-topped car and, as he got out, he left his codebook in a prominent position on the front seat. In our office the codebooks were kept in secure places and stamped 'Top Secret'. Wasn't that silly? It is no wonder that our convoy losses were so high early in the Battle of the Atlantic because the Germans could read our codes but we could not read theirs. Once the clever people based as Bletchley Park cracked the Enigma Code then the balance of power shifted and we could sink U-boats faster than they could build them. Our convoy losses were much reduced in consequence.*

It was not only the British who were intent upon keeping their military developments secret. The Germans were developing the first helicopters and testing a huge aircraft capable of carrying as many as 200 troops which could have played a vital role in the event of an invasion of Britain. They had also devised a cutting device which was fitted to aircraft and intended to sever the cables of barrage balloons. Fortunately, the British spies were aware of this and orders went out to vary the heights and positions of the barrage balloons. The leader of each balloon crew, usually an RAF NCO, was given secret orders day by day which were put into operation when an air raid was imminent. He was told where to position his balloon and the precise height at which it was to be flown. This meant that the German aircrews could not prepare their bombing maps in advance and, thus, the cable cutting programmes were abandoned.

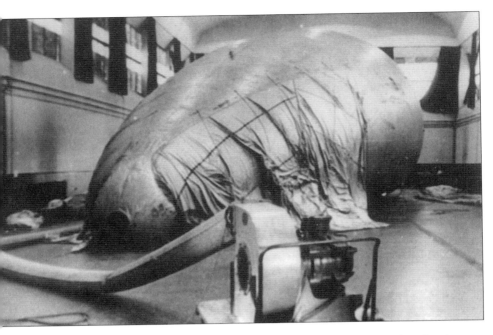

A barrage balloon on test. Thousands of these were produced and some were even exported to America.

The British also had their own secret failure which soon had to be abandoned as part of the barrage balloon defensive system. This involved attaching barrage balloons to ships in order to prevent aircraft from approaching too close. In the early days, however, the balloons were filled with hydrogen and if they were hit and fell onto the ship it could explode and this would have been catastrophic.

The positioning of barrage balloons in the regions was very carefully mapped. In Cheshire there were 949 balloons placed around Crewe, 923 around Runcorn and at Cuerdley near Warrington there were 922. There were a further 919 in the air above Birkenhead. Each balloon was connected by means of a mobile winch onto which was wrapped up to 3,000 ft of cable.

Another German device known as a 'butterfly' bomb was a small weapon dropped from aircraft. It fluttered down and was devised to attract the attention of civilians, especially children. There were fatalities from these bombs exploding but the censors worked efficiently and the figures were hidden so well that the Germans decided that they weren't being effective and so abandoned their use.

These days we tend to take early warning systems and electronic devices for granted. At the start of the war radar was very much in the experimental stage. A chain of radar stations was positioned around the coast to provide advance warning of approaching enemy aircraft but in the early days the system also indicated the presence of allied aircraft and the system had to be backed up by watchers. This, of course, presented problems during the hours of darkness. Eventually, an identification system known as the IFF system (Identification Friend or Foe) was developed. A system had been developed in 1935 called Chain

Barrage balloons soon became a familiar sight in Cheshire.

This butterfly bomb landed on the railway track.

Home Radar but initially this was concentrated along the coastline of the south-east of England. As war loomed, the system was enlarged and included some protection to the Mersey estuary.

At this time the radar stations worked in close association with the Royal Observer Corps. The Cheshire Control region which included Lancashire and what is now Cumbria was at first controlled from Barton Hall in Preston. The system, however, was soon relocated to the Woodvale sector. The early system was designed to locate aircraft only but later a Chain Low system was developed which was able to detect enemy shipping and was controlled from Derby House in Liverpool.

Whilst the radar and radio communications were improving, there was an initial reliance on the skills of the men and women who made up the Royal Observer Corps (ROC). They had to be both intelligent and well-informed and able to distinguish German aircraft from friendly by both sight and sound.

By 1940 an efficient network of observers was operating in the south-east of England but it soon developed all over the country, including Cheshire. They were organised by Alarm Officers and Alarm Controllers, the latter in direct contact with hundreds of keen observers. Illustrated notes were issued for guidance, books were published and newspapers like the *Sunday Dispatch* produced drawings of enemy aircraft. Tom Jenkinson remembers collecting these publications. He told me,

> *I was eleven in 1941 and I now know that kids, especially lads, had different views on the war than the adults. We wanted to test our knowledge of German bombers by seeing some but our elders were terrified of the bombs they were carrying. I never went anywhere without my Aircraft Recognition book which had cost me sixpence.*

Meanwhile the 'professionals' were setting up secret observation posts and naturally high ground provided the best sites. In Cheshire, the ROC used the network of existing Iron Age forts including those at Helsby, Bradley, Woodhouses, Eddisbury,

Some of the publications produced to help with aircraft identification.

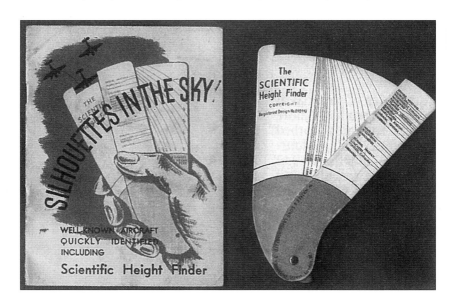

Oakmede, Kelsbarrow and the huge one of Maiden Castle. Use was also made of the Norman castles at Aldford, Beeston, Chester, Dunham Massey, Halton, Malpas and Stocklach. Another ideal ROC post was Mow Cop castle which was actually a folly built by Randle Wilbraham as a viewpoint looking over his home at Rode Hall which is now run efficiently by the National Trust.

There was also one branch of the ROC which is not often mentioned but which was important in areas around the rivers Mersey and the Dee. Some 1,500 members of the ROC were co-opted into the Merchant Navy as part of the DEMS project (Defensively Equipped Merchant Ships). They were known as Seaborne Observers and they played an important part in the War of the Atlantic and later during the Normandy invasion.

Land-based observers were present in areas approaching the Royal Ordnance factories, including those close to Risley and Hooton. High buildings were also important as observation points and the church towers around Cheshire were ideal. Among those used were at St Mary's, Astbury; St James's at Audlem; St Andrew's, Bebington; All Saints, Daresbury; St Mary's and All Saints at Great Budworth; St Oswald's at Lower Peover; and St James and St Paul's at Marton.

The Royal Ordnance Corps had a vital role to play as the Germans decided to blitz the towns and cities of Britain. These attacks placed the Civil Defence under great strain. Whilst the majority of the raids were directed at the big cities, Cheshire, too, had its cross to bear and the anti-aircraft batteries were on full alert. One large anti-aircraft post was on the site of Thurstaston Visitor Centre. This was number H28 anti-aircraft gun site which was a vital cog in the defensive ring protecting Liverpool. It is still possible to see the prominent but now landscaped mounds which mark the former gun emplacements. The off-duty crews were based in an area now occupied by a holiday park.

As was the case everywhere early in the war, the heavy hand of the censor prevented the true details from being published. It is only in recent years that a few accurate details have filtered

Mow Cop, used as an ROC observation point during the war.

through. We now know for certain that in the raids of 1940 and 1941, a total of 1,005 people were killed in Manchester and 4,100 in Liverpool and Merseyside, including the Wirral. To reach these areas the enemy bombers passed over Cheshire and Dorothy Hodkinson remembers these times very well,

> *During the Blitz I lived in Warrington which was on the bombers' flight path. At work we lost a lot of production time as we cowered in shelters while the German aircraft droned away above us. Apart from the sirens which were vital at night, we also had a daytime 'Imminent' warning sign which was a flag on top of our local brewery. We took it in turns to keep a look out for the flag. One night there was a huge blaze as an incendiary bomb hit a paint warehouse and the fire could be seen for miles around. This was targeted by more bombers and we took a bit of a battering. The following week they came back and they narrowly missed the parish church but demolished a row of old cottages which were of great historical interest. Next to our factory was a furniture shop which was completely gutted.*

All these events were carefully censured and the reports which were published in newspapers described the bombing of a northern town as suffering little damage and only a few casualties. ARP wardens had to report after each shift to fill in a form but they were not allowed to reveal a single detail. 'Serious' blitz attacks were particularly heavily censored. It is obvious that the events endured by Dorothy Hodkinson would never have been reported even though the raids were carefully documented. Dorothy continued,

> *I remember a lovely sunny Saturday when I left home to play tennis with a friend and then go to the pictures. What happened next made such an impression on me that I even remember what was on. It was all about an American*

Dorothy Hodkinson (far right) in 1940.

musician called Stephen Foster who wrote Jeannie with the Light Brown Hair *and* Camptown Races. *Just before the picture began, a notice was flashed up on the screen which read, 'Would any doctors, nurses or any persons with a knowledge of first aid, firemen or auxiliary workers of any type, please go at once to the Thames Board Mills and would the rest of the public keep away. Later I found out that my father had witnessed what happened. A lone German bomber had dropped several bombs in the midst of a crowd of people at a gala day at the Thames Board Mills. The mayor had previously begged them to cancel the event but it went ahead. My father told me that people were buried beneath marquees or blown across a meadow and many were killed. He remembered a baby being blown out of its pram and surviving but its mother was killed. He saw the plane dive down and drop its bombs and the event affected him for the rest of his life. I was determined to do something to help and I joined the Women's Land Army and served for four years.*

Sixteen people died but once again, the censor kept the fatalities very much a secret. It seems certain that the bomber had not aimed at the gala. In those days, bombing was not an accurate science and the crew had been seeking out a strategic target which may well have been the Ordnance factory at nearby Risley.

At times like this the emergency services were at full stretch and whilst most of the ARP wardens were volunteers, some were paid workers. A sign of the times was that men were paid £3. 5s. 0d. per week, while the women were paid only £2. An appeal for volunteers had first gone out in 1937. Whilst the uptake was very slow at first, it dramatically increased once war began. The ARP was officially described as 'a locally embedded service' which really meant that the wardens were expected to have an in-depth knowledge of their own area and to know most of the local inhabitants by name since they actually lived amongst them.

The wardens were organized into areas and there was a centrally-controlled recording office plus a back-up if this unit itself was put out of operation. At the end of each shift, a secret detailed report form had to be filled in. Various information points known as IPs were set up and once an incident was reported Rescue Squads were rushed in. These teams had a prominent letter R on their helmets and their overalls. Stretcher parties were also marked, in this case with the letters SP.

Casualties were labelled rather like luggage and on these was a note indicating death or a brief description of their injuries. There were also groups of very brave individuals who had volunteered literally to sweep up body parts!

Although civilian casualties were high, they were but a fraction of what the authorities had expected and the huge store of cardboard coffins and the designated mass graves all over Britain's towns and cities were thankfully not required. Even so, between 1940 and 1946, many wardens and other rescue crews were killed, some by previously unexploded bombs.

Another branch of the Civil Defence Service which toiled bravely during the Blitz was the Fire Service. The Blitz proved beyond all doubt that a co-ordinated fire service was urgently needed. Prior to the war there were only 5,000 full-time firemen in the whole of England, plus 50,000 auxiliaries who had other jobs but rushed to help in the event of a fire.

When Fire Officer Jim Riley, of Colne, was sent to Manchester during the Blitz his appliance returned with the paint peeled off because of the heat and the crew with singed eyebrows. Whilst he was there, he met Fire Officer Dan Williams, of Cheshire. They soon discovered that it was not possible to co-ordinate their work because their equipment had different specifications and so could not be coupled together.

Another problem was that when a bomb fractured a water main there was an obvious shortage of water and the fires could not then be brought under control. One solution was to position huge inflatable pools but even then the rubber from which they were made would often melt in the heat. Winnie Powell remembers these pools with affection,

> *My dad was a fireman in Stockport and he was given a supply of inflatable emergency pools which was kept in a converted hearse. He had a radio and if this was out of action a messenger was sent on a bike to tell him where the mains had been smashed. He looked for another source of water and the pools were placed on a lorry or a horse and*

cart and moved to where they were needed. These contraptions may not have worked very well but we loved ours. In 1946 my dad asked what he should do with the pools and he was told to dump 'em. He put one in our back garden and we kids had a lovely time in our paddling pool during the boiling hot summer of 1947.

All over Cheshire, supplementary fire stations were built with the obvious intention of assisting the full-time brigades. One which still exists is the St John's Road fire station at Handbridge which is close to Chester. It is in the grounds of Queens Park High School and is now used as a groundsman's storage hut. It was probably built to house only fire engines because the crew were local men who could be easily contacted in a hurry.

The prominent letters EWS (denoting the location of an emergency water supply) were painted on walls, pavements and buildings to assist the fire-fighters and a large letter H indicated the positions of hydrants. In many places, including Chester, the letters EWS are still visible; they can be seen on the Grosvenor Hotel and in Souters Lane, Frodsham Street and at the City Baths, as well as along Queens Park Road in Handbridge.

One event which even shocked experienced fire-fighters occurred on 3rd March 1941. A burning barrage balloon broke free of its moorings and came to rest on the deck of SS *Malakand* which was packed with thousands of tons of bombs. The whole load exploded and destroyed Huskisson dock in Liverpool and also killed several people. The flash and the explosion were seen in Birkenhead where the town itself was being bombed and 28 people killed. John Erickson recalled,

My uncle was an air raid warden in Birkenhead at the time but he never mentioned these events. All he said was that he filled in his duty form and said nowt. I also had an aunt who worked in the explosive works at Risley near Warrington and she wondered if she had helped to pack the bombs which exploded on the Malakand.

Firemen like Jim Riley and Dan Williams worked together during the Manchester Blitz but some of their equipment had difference dimensions which didn't make their jobs easy.

The auxiliary fire station at Handbridge which is now used as a school 'garden shed'.

Much work which often went unnoticed was done by the police. Along with their usual duties, they also had to direct traffic in the blackout for which officers were provided with white gloves and jackets. One set of statistics which was kept very secret during the war was that initially the crime rate rose markedly. A small, but very significant group of people did use the blitz and the sirens as a cover for criminal activity. The police had an unenviable task and Reg Hall of Liverpool was very much on the other side of the fence. He often travelled over the river to Birkenhead and said,

> *I was prepared to live for the day and we took what we could. Whatever you nicked you could sell on the black market and the spivs were always well off.*

The docks and railway goods yards were lucrative targets especially in 1940 and 1941 and all the civil authorities were kept at full stretch. It took them some time to get to grips with the situation and shops which had been bombed were often looked after by army units or the home guard. The situation was not helped when huge numbers of Americans who had plenty of money to spend began flooding into the towns. There were criminal groups, often with women among them, who were always on the prowl for drunken Yanks.

At this time there was plenty of money changing hands and there was a master forger based in Manchester who had a team working all over the North-West. His name was Herbert Winstanley and he produced £10, £5 and especially £1 notes in their thousands; they were so good that it took an expert to distinguish them from genuine notes. The police did an excellent job in arresting him, putting him behind bars and destroying his machinery.

The people on the Wirral side of the Mersey were very sympathetic to the people in Liverpool and Manchester who had lost their homes in the blitz and 50,000 people were provided with temporary accommodation. This was organised with great efficiency by members of the Women's Voluntary Service (WVS). Their operation swung into action in 1938 and Stella Isaacs, Lady Reading, was put in charge. In the North-West, Miss Rachael Kay-Shuttleworth was asked to provide rest centres for those who were bombed out. Rachael recalls,

> *I was told that I would have to travel many miles and hold many meetings. I was speaking to a group in Chester when a lady asked if my age would be a problem because I would be bound to run out of energy. I replied that I was a woman who was also eleven years younger than Winston Churchill and that shut her up.*

Like Lady Reading, Rachael had lots of contacts among Girl Guide leaders, many of whom were well-off and had access to cars, some of them very large. These were soon converted into ambulances, emergency fire engines, and mobile canteens. The Guides also had lots of ladies who were reliable, adaptable and knew how to cook. Lists were made of bed spaces and buildings which could be used as emergency shelters. Rachael continued,

The master forger, Winstanley, with (opposite) some of the counterfeit notes he produced.

There were also lots of useful aspects which I picked up during my trips and my notebooks were bulging with contacts. You have to remember that in those days the roads were not very good, the cars not so reliable and filling stations were few and far between. I had to make lists of people with telephones, bicycles, horses, as well as Guides and Scouts who could signal using flags. Postmen and other people with a detailed knowledge of an area were listed and contacted. All this had to be done as secretly as possible. I also had to list high points to make sure that the R.O.C. had not missed any area of importance. I always made a point of wearing my WVS uniform at meetings because it encouraged others to wear theirs and, in any case, it saved my clothing coupons. At

*this time I helped to establish more than 200 units in the
north-west of England. This proved to be so successful that
I was asked to go to London to explain how we operated
and our programme was followed in other parts of the
country.*

It is impossible to overestimate the vital role played during the
war by voluntary workers such as wardens, WVS and, of course,
the Home Guard. Whilst many of us are entertained by the TV
comedy programme *Dad's Army*, it should be remembered that
many Home Guard units were actually a very formidable fighting
force. There was always an extra incentive to fight when people
were defending their own homes and families. Walter Barnes
told me,

*There were several of us who were apprentice welders at
the Vicker's shipyard in Barrow and most of us worked on
submarines. One of my friends was Johnnie Hughes who
married a lass from Birkenhead and he got a job at
Cammell Laird. We kept in touch by letter until he died in
1979. When the war started, we were both miffed that we
couldn't join the forces because our work in the yard was
needed. Our way out was to join what was first called the
LDV but we were young and fit and did not intend to
'Look, Duck and Vanish'. We were not a joke or a Dad's
Army and we were glad when 'Winnie' Churchill changed
our name to the Home Guard. We did have some very
useful older chaps who had seen bullets fly in the First War
and they were an inspiration to all of us. Even after the
initial invasion threat had faded away, we still felt that
there was a threat. We bought copies of books and manuals
to help us and when I met up with Johnnie in 1947 at his
home near Birkenhead Priory he still had all his copies.
There was the Home Guard manual which could be bought
for a shilling and it gave instructions on map reading,
weapons, unarmed combat and ambush techniques.*

A Home Guard unit of railwaymen on duty.

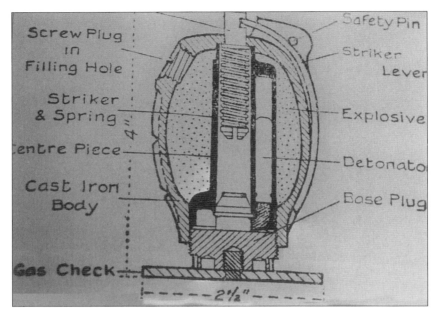

A diagram from a Home Front information leaflet showing the workings of a hand grenade.

Many units were recruited from within the works themselves. Who better to protect a railway than those who worked in and around them? Who better to protect a shipyard than the men who depended upon them for their work and pay? Johnnie Hughes was one of them,

> *Our unit was made up of men who had spent most of their working lives in the shipyards around the Wirral, plus a few others like postmen and schoolteachers. We soon knew how to service and fire weapons, including hand grenades, but what we were not good at was feeding ourselves. Unofficially at first but then with official blessing our ladies took a hand and things improved no end.*

All the Home Guard units knew how to protect their own patch and, if the worse came to the worst, they also knew how to destroy facilities in order to deny them to any invading force. In Cheshire and North Wales there were hundreds of tough quarrymen and miners who would have been a real threat, as Jeffrey Watkins related,

> *I worked in the slate mines in Snowdonia and I was asked to go to Chester where I and some other lads were met by a posh chap with shiny shoes and a lovely suit to sign the Official Secrets Act. I was asked if I could handle explosives and when I said yes I was told to go away with a map. I was to mark on it where explosives could be stored in secret places. If the invasion happened, we were to disappear into the bowels of the earth and wait for orders. These were never needed but I can assure you that we were ready.*

There were not just the regular Home Guard squads but also small units designed to make things difficult for an invading force. These units usually consisted of six or eight men who may well have had 'normal' jobs until they were called into action. They found existing holes or dug their own hideouts close to important sites. Once the code name *Cromwell* was used, then they were to go underground and prepare to inflict the maximum damage on the invading German forces.

The Germans reacted to the setting up of the Home Guard by declaring that these were not a military force but 'citizens in revolt' and would be executed on the spot. The Germans thought that this would be a deterrent but the reverse proved to be the case and recruitment increased threefold.

There was a 'secret rumour' that some Home Guard units were being given a supply of American weapons and ammunition. Apparently, a ship with a hold full of weapons that had been taken from the gangsters of the 1930s by the FBI had been handed over to the British, along with detailed instructions on how to use the weapons. Units all over Britain were trained in the use of German weapons which were of a different calibre to those used by the British Army. The idea was to take any weapons recovered from the German invaders and give them a bit of their own back.

Happily, the invasion never happened but Britain still had to endure bombardment from the air. The blitz caused misery to cities and towns across the land, especially London, Coventry, Bristol and Hull but Manchester and Liverpool took a pounding too, and Cheshire had its own blitz to cope with.

On 9th April 1941 bombs fell on Prenton Park, Birkenhead and, on the following day, high explosive bombs fell on Wallasey. Between September 1940 and May 1941 there were 68 'serious' raids on the area, as well as a number of isolated attacks which meant that people could not relax, especially as the dark of the night seemed to hold extra terrors. The May Blitz of 1941 led to many people not trusting the shelters as Mary Neild who lived in Birkenhead at the time told me,

My elder sister Sheila was a history teacher in Chester and she had a collection of pictures of Birkenhead Park. She and mum thought that places protected by rocks would be safer than our Anderson shelter in the back garden. We had an old pram with wobbly wheels and every night that May we packed it with blankets, sandwiches, our tea and sugar ration, milk and an old primus stove and headed for the park. I don't know if we were actually safer there in the park but it didn't matter because we felt safer.

The Government did make provision for shelters and various types were designed. Huge volumes of information were

Birkenhead Park where some families, like the Neilds, preferred to sit out the bombing rather than retreat to the air raid shelters.

produced. One such publication was *The Protection of Your Home Against Air Raids* which instructed people to designate a safe room and protect it the best way they could. What did that mean, I wonder? Another suggestion was that it was the duty of the head of the household to ensure that all gas masks were within easy reach. Thankfully, neither side used gas during the war and we now look at gas masks in a humorous light but businessmen did not lose the opportunity to produce masks for babies which

A GAS-PROOF KENNEL (with Air Filter).

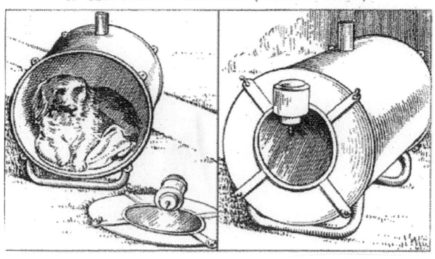

The National Canine Defence League developed a gas-proof kennel for dogs, and there was even one for horses too (see opposite page); whilst parents had to learn how to operate gas masks designed for babies.

covered the whole body, whilst those for children were constructed to look like the cartoon character Mickey Mouse. There were even masks for the use of dogs and cats. Comical posters were produced showing women talking over the garden wall whilst wearing their gas masks.

The police and Civil Defence Services were also trained on how to react to a gas attack. Decontamination centres were set up in most towns and cities but the only threat in the event came from bombs. There is no doubt that the shelters did work and from a household aspect the most effective was the Anderson shelter named after its inventor. It was of simple construction and made

Policemen dressed ready for a possible gas attack.

of sheets of corrugated iron and bolted together. A hole was dug into the ground and earth piled on top which gave an extra layer of protection. As part of the 'Dig for Victory' campaign, vegetables were grown on top of the soil on the shelter roof. Many people made their shelter comfortable and fitted bunks and paraffin lamps. They were always damp, however, and often flooded. After the war many were used as garden sheds and some are still in use to this day. Payment for the shelters was calculated after a means test. Those who could afford to paid but the poor didn't and old folk were provided with free labour to install them.

Many people, however, did not have gardens and this led to the invention of the Morrison shelter named after Herbert Morrison, the then Home Secretary. This was literally a strengthened table consisting of a steel top supported by firm legs and a framework covered in strong wire with a door which could be secured. Many people used the Morrison instead of a dining room table and a few adapted them for table tennis.

Far less popular were the brick-built commercial shelters which were erected in nearly every town street. Looked at in retrospect they were not a very efficient protection and most people would have been safer at home. In Stockport, though, there was one huge shelter, which was almost one hundred per cent safe. It consisted of a series of tunnels cut into the soft sandstone rock. These began to be constructed in 1938 and were opened in October 1939, and initially had spaces for 4,000 people. At first, local people thought that the system was a waste of money but once the London Blitz had pierced the mists of secrecy they realised the sense of the project and capacity was soon increased to 7,000. The network was fitted with bunk beds, electric lighting and a mix of chemical and main sewer toilets. Situated on Chestergate, it is now a museum. Log on to www.airraidshelters.org.uk or tel. 0161 474 1940 for further details.

Once it became obvious how safe and luxurious this shelter was, people came in from nearby Manchester and there was soon not enough room for residents. The result was that a ticket system was introduced and a few ticket touts developed a good business. The tunnels leading to the main shelters were 7 ft wide and there were ventilation shafts, a first-aid post and a warden's room. Although it cannot be proved with any certainty, there were also secret areas where confidential information was stored.

There were a number of types of bomb used by the Germans, each of which had to be dealt with differently. Some 80% of the bombs dropped were described as HEs, which meant high explosive types, but there were also a number of 'general purpose' bombs known as SCs after the German *Sprengbombe Cylindrisch*. Then there were incendiaries which were small and contained lots of phosphorous so that they started fires very easily. These were usually dropped so that the fires could guide the aircraft which followed. The British reacted by lighting fires in the open countryside, thus deceiving the night bombers into dropping their lethal loads in the wrong place. The Germans also dropped bombs which were about the size of a dustbin and consisted of oil, plus a fuse to ignite the weapon and keep it burning. Then there were the parachute bombs which were really large mines fitted with delayed-action fuses that exploded often hours after the bombers had departed. A particularly nasty type known as the butterfly bomb has already been mentioned in the previous chapter. The unexploded bomb teams (UXBs) did a wonderful job but between 1940 and 1947 no fewer than 490 of these brave people were killed and many more badly injured.

Many think that the V1s, better known as Doodlebugs, were only dropped on the London area and the south-east. In fact, some were aimed to pass over Hull and then onwards and inland. A few landed in the north-west, including Cheshire where they exploded in Garners Lane, Stockport, and others reached Hyde and Didsbury. The V1s were programmed to drop leaflets prior to impact and explosion. These contained messages supposedly written by British POWs pointing out that it was better living in Germany under Hitler than in Britain under Churchill. A blanket of secrecy descended and the leaflets were gathered up and burned whilst the V1 raids were not reported at all.

Chapter 3

Cheshire's Secret Sites

It was obvious to all in authority that the German tourists of the 1930s had done their job well and also that the Luftwaffe had conducted aerial sorties and knew the location of the main targets. With the technology then available, bombers could reach distant targets but the fighters did not have enough range to provide cover. The British came up with the concept of building dummy sites to persuade the German pilots to bomb in the wrong place.

These were all built in great secrecy and there were daytime decoys called 'K' sites whilst the night-time decoys were called 'Q' sites. The 'K' sites consisted of rows of tents and aircraft or tanks made of rubber or canvas. Members of the Magic Circle who performed in the music halls were contacted and encouraged to share their stagecraft illusions. Later, QF sites were developed which had fires that could be lit to indicate that bombing had already started. It did not take long for the plans to be adapted to protect factories and other vital installations.

Later, 'SF' sites were designed, known as Starfish sites. Since the end of the war, at least 170 of these sites have been identified, including some in and around Cheshire. Several installations in the Burtonwood area and around Warrington, including Risley Ordnance Factory, were protected in this way and there were also Starfish sites at Bold Heath, Hatton, Appleton and Arley. To protect Manchester there were decoy sites on Chat Moss, Carrington Moss and Tatton Park where General Patton was based. To protect Liverpool and Birkenhead docks there were Starfish sites at Heswall, Gayton, Burton Marsh, Brimstage and Wallasey, as well as at Llandegla and Llanas in North Wales.

These days it is very difficult to appreciate just how vital the Ordnance factories such as the one at Risley were. It was so important that a massive Starfish site was set up not so far away on a mossland area and it did confuse the German bomber crews. The 927-acre site was built as secretly and as quickly as possible and opened in September 1940. In the event, it was not a German bomber which caused a loss of life but an accident within the complex itself. Workers in one area were known as the Suicide Squad because of the number of accidents which took place. Sadie Black was blinded, sustained a badly-injured leg and had some fingers blown off as 450 detonators exploded. Mabel Dobson was a luckier member of the squad but has vivid memories of its dangers. Workers had to wear goggles and gloves and were visited regularly by Danger Building Inspectors to make sure that all safety rules were being followed. Modern-day Health and Safety inspectors would, however, have had the whole place closed down in an instant. Workers weighed explosives using simple household scales and then packed and sealed the detonators by hand. In the case of liquid explosives, these were poured into the weapons using large variations of oil cans or kettles!

Mabel remembers the air raid warnings which meant a rush for the shelters. Here the workers were often joined by sheep which were driven in by shepherds from the fields which surrounded the site.

It was not only detonators and fuses which were filled at Risley. Huge weapons, including the Grand Slam used by the

Dambusters, were filled at Risley and also at nearby Chorley. It is no wonder that both facilities had Starfish sites associated with them.

In 1946 the site was taken over by the United Kingdom Atomic Energy Authority, no doubt because there was already good security around the area. It did not stay long, however, and the site is now occupied by the Birchwood Park Office Complex and the area has become a popular nature reserve.

Apart from the Starfish Delusion Strategy, the British boffins were also working on techniques to disrupt the German bombers' navigational aids. The Germans had devised an ingenious method of guiding a bomber to a target. They produced two high-frequency radio transmitters which intersected on the target. The navigator followed a path between the beams and if it veered to the right a series of morse code dashes were recorded. If he veered to the left a series of morse code dots were picked up. When the two beams met the bombs were released. The system was known as *Knickebein* which literally meant 'crooked leg'; to the British it was known as Headache and their reaction to it was called Aspirin!

The British boffins' solution was to bend these beams and focus them either over the sea or onto a Starfish site. Among these boffins was Douglas Hartree who was Professor of Mathematics at Manchester University. One of his students at the time was Bernard Lovell who, after the war, took the lead in the construction of the Jodrell Bank radio telescope in Cheshire. Bernard Lovell, who died in 2012, was knighted in 1961 for his pioneering work in the field of radio astronomy. The Manchester team worked closely with the AVRO company at Woodford. One of their Ansons was adapted for use as a research aircraft. It was affectionately known as Aggy Paggy because of its registration letters G-AGPG.

The famous Aggy Paggy used to develop communications systems.

The British bomb boffins did not just concentrate on defence but they also devised plans to protect our bomber crews by disrupting the Germans' own radar. The British equivalent to *Knickebein* was called 'Oboe' and the Mosquito, Halifax, Wellington and Lancaster aircraft were used to drop pieces of silver paper called window chaff which caused the German communication systems to jam.

There were several other secret locations in Cheshire which needed protecting, including another Ordnance factory at Hooton, as well as the airfield at Ringway and the Bidston Observatory. It is interesting to note that Ringway was never officially taken over by the War Office but was always under the direction of Manchester City Council. This was obviously a very sophisticated cover up. Apart from being a centre for linguists being trained to parachute into enemy-occupied Europe, there were many other secret operations which were ongoing. There were trials taking place to perfect the use of gliders, as well as experiments to fit jet engines into bombers, including the Lancaster.

One fascinating experiment was the Hafner Rotachute which was a combination of a conventional parachute incorporated into a helicopter-like rotor, beneath which was a small fuselage. This was a real James Bond-like contraption and was still on the secret list in the 1970s. It is interesting to note that Ian Fleming, the author of the James Bond books, was also a member of the Secret Service during the war.

Many paratroopers were trained at Ringway and subsequently taken into the mountains of the Lake District to be toughened up. Their first operational sortie was the successful raid in May 1940 on a German radar station where their aim was to steal vital pieces of equipment. These first 120 men were made up of soldiers from the Black Watch, plus a London group known as the Piccadilly Allsorts.

Troops boarding a Horsa Glider. Many of the men trained at Ringway.

The same group was also active in the build-up to D-Day. As General Patton's bogus army based at Knutsford persuaded the Germans to concentrate on Calais rather than Normandy, these paratroopers based at Ringway went into northern England and Scotland. Enough information was leaked to persuade the Germans that the Allied invasion was to begin in Norway and then onwards through Denmark and into Germany. Because of these two diversions, the Germans kept many thousands of crack troops on high alert instead of sending them off to repel the landings in Normandy.

Even though we now know about Patton's mythical army, there are still many secrets which have yet to be unravelled. The Germans believed that Patton was the Allies' best Assault Commander and Patton himself was also convinced of that. This is why he was angry and frustrated when he found he was to be used as a decoy and would not be involved in the early days of the D-Day battles. He was a complex character who always overstepped the mark, while Montgomery on the British side was just as undiplomatic so it is no wonder the two hated each other.

Patton's almost fatal *faux pas* took place in Knutsford's Gothic town hall when he delivered an anti-Communist tirade against the Russians who were our allies at that time. Stalin was no diplomat himself and soon took offence. Patton's base was at Peover Hall which dates to 1585 and he often dined at the Whipping Stocks Hotel where there are photographs of him on display and the table where he dined is still in position. When he finally did leave for Normandy, he left money to provide flowers for his table.

Whilst General Patton was at Peover Hall, a huge dummy base close to Knutsford was built and a Starfish area was also produced nearby. Alex Murray recalls his work as a carpenter on the dummy base,

Lots of buildings were under construction but as far as I know none of them were actually finished. This

led us all to believe that there would be no invasion until the summer of 1946. We were totally surprised to find out after Normandy that the invasion was on and had taken place without General Patton. We had all been part of a massive confidence trick which I can only describe as brilliant.

The telephone lines around the site were kept constantly busy and 'secret' documents were deliberately leaked. Some troops, apparently drunk, provided lots of loose talk and kept referring to Calais. The trick obviously worked and even after the Normandy landings, hundreds of tanks were kept idle in the Calais area. The Starfish-type strategy was codenamed *Operation Bodyguard* and it involved the use of inflatable tanks, light wooden glider mock-ups and even some dummy troops in battle dress.

It was not just new sites which had to be given the camouflage treatment for there were other sensitive places which needed to be protected. One of these was the Bidston Observatory. This had been built in 1867 to provide a viewpoint from which shipping could be observed on its way into Liverpool. Signals could then be sent by means of semaphore to an area in Liverpool still known as Exchange Flags. This meant that merchants knew when their cargo was arriving and their sales teams were prepared. The nearby windmill was used by the ROC as an important viewing point whilst the Observatory building below was given the maximum protection.

This was because, at the time of the war, a really reliable Tidal Predicting Machine had been developed. During the 1980s, whilst presenting a television programme, I was able to view this wonderful machine at close quarters. It had 5,000 gears and 42 pulley wheels which were sensitive to the gravitational pull of the sun, moon and each of the planets. It was used to accurately predict the time and range of the tides at any point of the globe and was accurate to within one tenth of one degree. In the 1960s the machine was replaced by a computer but this is not quite as accurate. During the war vital data was provided especially during

One of the thousands of inflatable tanks used in Operation Bodyguard.

the build up to D-Day and the Americans also made some use of the machine during their Pacific campaign. The secrets of its use were obviously protected as it was never attacked. The same can be said of the PLUTO project but this was by no means a 'Mickey Mouse' operation.

The PLUTO oil pipeline was so long and so well organised that it sounds more like fiction than fact. A reliable supply of oil was essential at all times but especially in the build up to and following the Normandy landings. A pipeline ran under the sea from the Isle of Wight to the beaches with the control centre disguised as an old ice-cream factory. Obviously there were no harbour facilities in the Isle of Wight and so an underground and under-the-sea pipeline was connected to all of the west coast harbours as far north as Liverpool. A large and specially designed unloading area

The Tidal Predicting Machine at Bidston (above), with (left) one of the dials enlarged. In its day, this huge machine was the world leader in calculating the rise and fall in tides all over the world.

was constructed in the Mersey and a pipeline dug throughout the length of the country. Amos Chapel told me,

> *My father lived near Marple and got a job which he thought was digging drains to repair the damage done by the blitz in Liverpool. When he died in 1976 he was still unaware of the exact nature of the work he did. He did say, though, that the pipes which were being laid didn't look like drains. Don't you find it amazing that the PLUTO project remained a secret for all those years and that the Mersey section was just a part of a massive secret jigsaw?*

Much of Cheshire at the time of the war could be described as an armed camp and it was vital to keep as much under wraps as possible. The bases in the county were important both to the war at sea and in the air.

| Chapter 4 |

The War on Land and in the Air

Those who think that Cheshire had only a minor role to play during the Second World War are very much mistaken. In the case of Warrington, the whole place was a focal point of the war effort and it is no exaggeration to say that the town and the surrounding area was an armed camp. Malcolm Hopkins who now lives in St Albans recalls,

I was twelve in 1943 and Warrington was buzzing with soldiers, airmen and even some navy chaps from RAF Stretton. The town at that time was famous for its breweries but even so there was often a shortage of beer. There was a huge American base at Burtonwood and the Yanks soon got used to drinking pints of warm beer with a froth on top. My dad worked in a wireworks and told me that the local foundry workers were always thirsty and there was a bit of a battle if the beer ran out. He said that we would have lost the war if booze and fags had run out.

Apart from the 10,000 Americans at Burtonwood, there was an RAF basic training unit at Padgate on the edge of Warrington. Padgate was known as No 3 RAF depot and was opened in 1939. By 1943 the weekly intake was 1,500. The camp closed in 1957 and the site was redeveloped. There was a British Army base at the Peninsular Barracks on O'Leary Street, Warrington, which later became a base for the local Territorial Army. In addition, there was an RAF and Fleet Air Arm station at nearby Appleton Thorn.

For centuries, Warrington had been an important focal point for transport as here was a major crossing point over both the River Mersey and the Manchester Ship Canal. The town was also an important producer of steel but, especially, a manufacturer of wire which was of vital importance during the war. Until recently the Warrington Wolves Rugby League Club was known as the 'Wires' and some supporters still hark back to the original name. Jane Manningham who lived in Chester until her death in 2008 told me,

My father-in-law was a policeman in Warrington and he was told to learn about the history of the Wires so that he could question strangers who may well have been spies. When the Americans arrived he had to learn about baseball, basketball and boxing, too.

Apart from the camps, there was also a unit based at Marbury Hall which dates to the 13th century but which was substantially remodelled in the 1850s. In the Second World War it was used as a military camp and at one time housed some of the survivors from Dunkirk. Audrey Shilton who still lives in Manchester told me,

My father was at Dunkirk and he was sent to Marbury to get his head together. We were living in Birkenhead at the time and he was given leave to visit us. He never ever talked about Dunkirk and his mates were told not to mention it either. The only time he ever showed any emotion was when he saw a fishing trawler. After the war he always wore a cap and when he saw a trawler he would call out 'Thanks, lads'. We were once on holiday in Fleetwood and he was doffing his cap all the time. It turned out that he was transported from Dunkirk in a trawler.

Towards the end of the war, the camp at Marbury was converted to a Prisoner of War camp. One of the most famous of the inmates was a German paratrooper called Bert Trautmann. After a period of working on a farm and then in bomb disposal, Bert achieved fame as Manchester City's goalkeeper. I once heard him say, 'I feel more English than German. Here you have freedom in every sense of the word and the people in and around Marbury Camp were so kind that I was glad that we lost the war.'

Sadly, Marbury Hall was demolished in 1968 after being used as a hostel for Polish workers employed by ICI who, like Bert Trautmann, chose to remain in England after the war.

Like Warrington, Chester was also an armed camp. Two miles from the city, along the B5130, is Saighton where an army camp was built in 1940. What was unusual is that the construction was dogged by industrial disputes. These seem to have revolved around the living conditions and allowances which did not satisfy the workers. Things soon settled down, however, and the camp was quickly completed.

From Saighton, thousands of soldiers trekked out into the local countryside to complete endurance training but the lads did have some time to relax. They had their own cinema and a theatre where ENSA ('Every Night Something Awful') artists trod the boards. Henry Longhurst who later became a famous golf commentator was among the young men who trained there.

During the war, there is no doubt that Cheshire's most important industry was aviation and the Fairey Aviation's Heaton Chapel works near Stockport played an important role. It was set up as a shadow factory for the Bristol Aviation Company in 1937. The company's most famous aircraft at this time was the Fairey Swordfish which first flew in 1934, entered service with the RAF in 1936 and was the last bi-plane to see action. By 1943 the Fleet Air Arm had realised that the model was obsolete but it was not taken out of service completely until 1946. In 1940, the Swordfish carried out a successful raid from aircraft carriers during the engagement at Taranto against the Italian fleet and helped with the destruction of the German battleship *Bismark* in 1941 whilst flying off from the deck of the *Ark Royal*.

The Swordfish, known affectionately by airmen as the 'Stringbag' had an open cockpit which meant that the two-man crew were always cold. It was powered by a Bristol Pegasus engine as Jim Ashton recalled,

I worked on assembling Pegasus engines all through the war. I was mainly based at a factory at Clayton-le-Moors, near Accrington but was often sent to help when engines were being fitted and tested at the Stockport works. Our engines had to be powerful because slung underneath the stringbag was a huge torpedo. I do remember being told not to mention the details of the sling holding the torpedo. This meant secret modifications to the undercarriage as the torpedoes got heavier.

After the war, the Cheshire factory was taken over by the Westland Aircraft Company based at Yeovil in Somerset and they soon began to specialize in the production of helicopters. The company was interested in the Fairey Rotodyne system which had been developed at Heaton Chapel and tested at Ringway.

The Stockport factory was also involved in modifications to the Beaufighter plane. Once the engineers were happy with the engine modifications, the aircraft were sent on to the Samlesbury

The Fairey Swordfish, whose engines were fitted at Stockport. Just by looking at the machine you can see why its crews called it 'Stringbag'!

Engineering Company near Preston. Here top secret radio and radar systems were installed. The engines had been tuned to such a fine pitch that the Beaufighter was called *Whispering Death*. Pat Young told me,

> *My father worked on the fine-tuning of the Beaufighter and was visited by Donald Campbell. After the war my*

father was asked by Donald to work on his Bluebird speedboat and we all spent many a happy day around Coniston Water.

Shadow factories were the brainchild of the aircraft minister Lord Beaverbrook and his idea was to have aircraft production based at several sites so that if one factory was bombed the whole production would not be affected. The Broughton factory on the

Pat Young's father, Norman, who worked on the Beaufighter plane.

The Bristol Beaufighter, nicknamed 'Whispering Death'.

outskirts of Chester was another shadow factory that played a vital role during the war. It was built to produce Wellington bombers which were affectionately known as *Wimpys* after the cartoon character of the time, J. Wellington Wimpy. The design was based on the technique developed by Barnes Wallis when working on airships in the 1930s. It involved using very lightweight alloys and developing a framework of Meccano-like struts covered by fabric which became known as the geodetic structure.

The Broughton shadow factory eventually employed 8,000 people, of whom a high proportion were women. In 1940 there was a publicity project to break the world record by assembling an aircraft from start to flight in 24 hours. The number was LN514 and a film was made of the operation, with an American voice-over in order to encourage those over the water to join in the hostilities. At its peak, the factory was producing 28 Wellingtons every week. More Wellingtons were produced during the war than any other bomber, including the later, more famous, Lancaster.

Workers were attracted to work at Broughton from all over Cheshire and North Wales, including Hilda Dodd who had worked in a local photographer's shop before 'developing' an interest in the war. Another employee, Betty Weaver, remembers being fitted out with a white boiler suit and the shop floor looking more like a hospital ward than an aircraft factory; whilst Bob Wilson recalls being brought up to believe that only men could produce aircraft but that the women at Broughton proved him wrong. Tiny Cooling was a pilot who said that the Wellington was a large lump of engineering genius. He flew 65 missions in the aircraft which was 65 ft long and had an 80 ft wingspan. 'The only place that plane belonged' said Tiny 'was in the air'. Bill Anderson started working at Broughton when he was fourteen and remarked:

One day I was a child scouring the countryside and getting pocket money and the next I was a man earning a wage.

Workers outside the Broughton factory in November 1940 crowding around a Wellington bomber.

The assembly line at the Broughton shadow factory.

Some incendiary bombs did drop close to the factory and Eileen Lyndfield remembers heading to the shelters which had wooden seats and a table on which stood a wind-up gramophone but only one record. It was a 78 rpm of Gracie Fields singing *The Biggest Aspidistra in the World*. Eileen worked an 8-hour shift and still has fond memories of the canteen which served chips followed by rice pudding. Miss Littler was one of the supervisors looking after the welfare of the girls who were stitching the fabric into the airframe prior to having the dope smeared onto it. This smelled like nail varnish and often made people feel sick. The girls had to produce eight neat stitches to the inch, evenly spaced, and their work was very carefully checked. If it was not right, then the work had to be unpicked and done again. They were allowed a maximum of six minutes for a toilet break.

Many of the girls had friends or relatives in the RAF and they knew that if they did not do their jobs properly, then the *Wimpy* would be less reliable and lives would be lost. Making every stitch count really did have relevance for these girls. Eileen Lyndfield remembers that there was one perk attached to the job

Lots of little bits of fabric went to waste when making the airframes and these bits could be taken home and made into slippers.

Ernest Tootal worked on the new bomb hatch and the landing wheel mechanism for the Wellington, while Robert Davies worked on a crane. Wilf Williams drove a tractor which moved the bomber from the assembly area to the hangers prior to flight testing. All these people were well aware of the sensitive nature of the work they were doing at Broughton.

Unlike many of the wartime sites, Broughton is still there. Just after the war, the factory produced some of the parts used to construct pre-fabricated houses and now it is a vital component in the network which produces the huge European Airbus, the largest civilian aircraft in the world.

During and after the war there were many companies producing aircraft and, so far as Cheshire was concerned, the huge AVRO factory at Woodford was by far the largest. Initially the AVRO Company was Lancashire-based but it soon became obvious that an area was needed as a flying base and in 1925 a new facility was built at Woodford. It was here that the famous AVRO 504s were produced. From 1930 onwards the RAF had realised that whatever some of the politicians were saying, war was inevitable and victory in the air would be essential. AVRO needed even more space and a new purpose-built factory was constructed at Chadderton, near Oldham. Harry Holmes, the eminent historian and the former publicity officer at AVRO told me,

The new complex at Chadderton became a design centre and the final assembly and flight testing was carried out at Woodford and this was massively extended for this purpose.

80

The Germans were well aware of these units but despite this, neither factory was badly damaged during hostilities. It would seem that the beam bending boffins and the Starfish deceptions had done their work well. Charlie Wilson who worked at Woodford told me an interesting story,

> *Because there were such close links between us and the folks at Chadderton, we knew that one bomb had hit part of their factory. It hit the screw, nuts and bolts store and all the different sizes became jumbled up together. It was going to take ages to sort them out until somebody had the bright idea to recruit the local blind people. They did it by touch and they were brilliant at it.*

Very contrasting machines – the ill-fated Manchester and the legendary Lancaster – were produced from these two factories. Eddie Talbot remembers working on the Manchester,

> *I had just finished my apprenticeship when they started to make the Manchester and the bomber looked to us to be a*

Avro aircraft at Woodford in 1939: (left to right) Auto Giro C3A, Avro 626 and an Avro Anson.

The Anson assembly line at Newton Heath in 1936. Over 11,000 Avro Ansons were built for the RAF from 1936 to 1952. Many more were later exported.

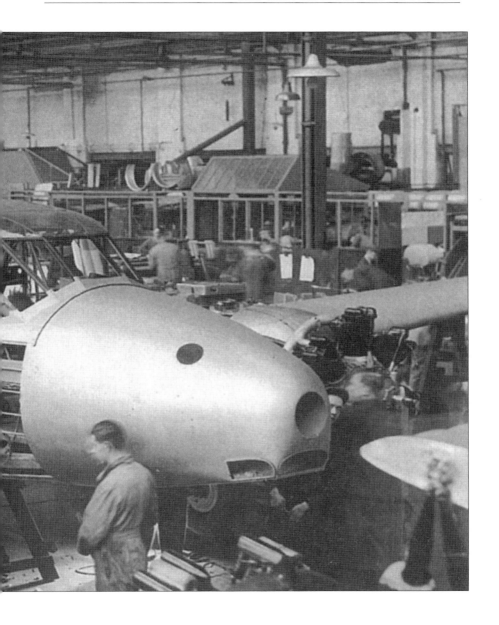

real winner but we were young and over-optimistic. It soon became obvious that it had two major flaws. The airframe was fine but there were only two engines and for once the Rolls Royce engines were not very good. The Air Ministry were about to cancel the whole project which would have been a disaster for the AVRO factories. The chief designer Roy Chadwick went down to London and blew his top. He persuaded the powers at the top that he would increase the wing span to allow for four engines and insisted that Rolls Royce Merlin engines were fitted. Those of us who worked on the Lancaster knew that it was by far the best bomber which flew in the war.

I am convinced that what he says is correct. The Germans never managed to develop a four-engine aircraft capable of carrying the bomb load of the Lancaster which successfully delivered the huge Tallboy and Grand Slam bombs which destroyed the dams of the Ruhr Valley and other strategic targets. Woodford continued to play a vital role in aircraft construction until it was finally shut down in 2010.

The Manchester prototype on display at Ringwood.

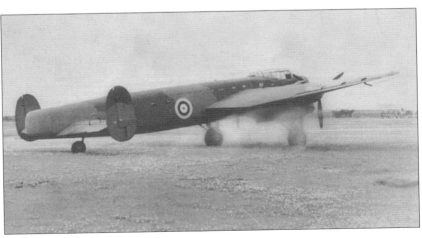

The Rolls Royce Vulture engine installed in the Manchester proved to be a disaster.

Woodford and the Lancaster and Broughton and the Wimpy will never be forgotten but there are some airfields in Cheshire which have almost – but thankfully not quite – been forgotten. One of these is at Hooton Park which had first been constructed in 1917 to train pilots for the Royal Flying Corps (later renamed the RAF) but the station was closed down in 1919. It fell into disuse until 1929 when a band of enthusiasts formed the Liverpool and District AVRO club. It was visited by many famous aviators, including Amy Johnson. For a short period Hooton Park was the only commercial airfield in the north of England and preceded Speke (now John Lennon Liverpool) and Ringway (now Manchester International). Hooton was the official Liverpool airport until Speke took over in 1933. In 1936 the Number 610

(County of Chester) Squadron of the RAF was set up at Hooton and during the war it was taken over by Coastal Command and patrolled an area from South Wales to the Irish Sea. It worked in conjunction with the experimental Anson aircraft *Aggy Paggy*.

At Hooton there was also a small assembly factory run by Martin Hearn. He was something of an eccentric character who, as a young man, had been a wing walker with Cobhams Flying Circus. After the war, this factory was still assembling aircraft but it finally closed down in 1957; in 1962 the site was purchased by the Vauxhall Car Company and vehicles are still being produced there.

Hooton was a small site in comparison to Burtonwood which is situated 2½ miles south of Warrington. This became the largest American airbase in Europe and was the first to open and the last to close. The United States military were there until 1993 but it lost its main impetus once the Cold War had thawed. By 2004 much of the site had been built over but street names recall the era with names such as California Drive and Dakota Park, whilst Moran Drive is a reminder of one of the most popular of the base commanders.

Burtonwood originated as an RAF site and was chosen because there were good road and railway links close by; there was also a large reservoir of labour wanting work in the 1930s. It was in 1936 that the RAF began to construct an Aircraft Repair Depot (ARD) and it was greatly expanded from 1938 onwards. It was placed under the control of the Ministry of Aircraft Production. We know from their records that the Luftwaffe did have photographs of the site under construction but it was never seriously damaged by bombs. It may have been because the Germans thought that Liverpool and Manchester were more important targets but it could have also been that the Starfish sites and the bending beam boffins had done their work well.

Burtonwood had an American connection from the early days as the Lend-Lease scheme involved the delivery of aircraft to Liverpool docks for onward transport by road to the air base. Once the Americans joined the war Burtonwood was turned over to them and up to 10,000 men were working on the site, including Barney Connolly who told me how he got used to living in England,

It took time to get used to the coinage – the huge heavy copper pennies with the King's head on the top, the half pennies with a ship on the back and the tanners, bobs and quids. I hope you don't mind me using the word but I was amazed at how patient you Limeys were – and still are – you queue without pushing in. Your sense of humour also confused us young Yanks to begin with. If you insulted us, it was a sign that you liked us and were not trying to pick a fight.

There were lots of well-kept secrets involved with Burtonwood, including the Turbinlite Havocs which were used as a defence against bombers. These were Douglas Boston twin-engined bombers, with a Turbinlite searchlight fitted into the nose, which flew at night, accompanied by a fighter. The Boston illuminated an enemy bomber and then the fighter homed in on it and shot it down. This strategy was kept very secret but, surprisingly, it was not very successful and was discontinued. The aircraft flew from Burtonwood and linked up with fighters from RAF Woodvale on the Lancashire side of the Mersey.

The Carpetbagger Project was also top secret and involved using specially-adapted B24 bombers to fly agents trained at Ringway into German-occupied Europe under cover of darkness. The bombers had had their nose gun turret removed and the whole aircraft was painted black. This proved to be very effective against enemy searchlights and this strategy was in continual use until the end of the war.

The Aphrodite Scheme involved stripping out all non-essential equipment from B17s and packing them with explosives. They were fitted with remote, radio-controlled, automatic pilot. Their purpose was to fly into specific targets such as the coastal U-boat pens which were almost impossible to destroy by the conventional

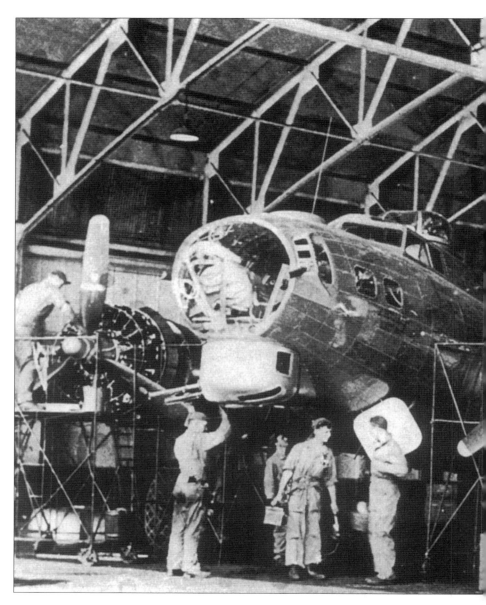

A B-17 bomber being serviced at Burtonwood in 1944.

bombs then in use, until Barnes Wallis devised his 'bouncing' bomb. The aircraft, accompanied by a mother aircraft, took off with just a 'normal' pilot on board. The bomb aircraft pilot would then bale out and be picked up at sea whilst his aerial bomb was then radio-guided by the mother aircraft onto the target. At that time radio-controlled weapons were very much in their infancy and there were fatalities, including that of Joseph Patrick Kennedy, the brother of John F. Kennedy who would later become president of the United States.

The CF-4A WACO glider was another well-kept Burtonwood secret and again it worked in close association with Ringway. This was just a simple glider fitted with a couple of small engines to allow some semblance of control. This was not very successful and was soon discontinued but there were other glider developments being carried out at Ringway, including the Patterson single-seater which could be launched from beneath the aircraft which delivered it. It was successfully used in Norway. One very secret project which went on at Burtonwood involved adapting aircraft to be used to ferry General Patton and General Eisenhower to important meetings.

The first American personnel arrived at Burtonwood on 11th June 1942. All the bases were given RAF status and were officially 'loaned' to the Americans. What was actually going on was kept as secret as possible. The sound of the engines being tested could be heard all over Warrington but the local people were never fully in the picture.

Around the Burtonwood site there were four miles of railway track which was linked to the main line. At the end of the war the site occupied 1250 acres (500 hectares) and this is quite astounding because it was originally designed to cater for only 648 RAF personnel. Eventually there were 1,823 buildings and as many as 10,000 men who all needed feeding, billeting and entertaining. Hollywood stars made regular visits to a purpose-built theatre on the site including Bing Crosby, Bob Hope and James Cagney (but not James Stewart who was too busy flying a B-17 himself). There were the big dance bands of the RAF

Glenn Miller and his band at Burtonwood in August 1944; four months later, on the way to France, the aircraft he was flying disappeared, and he was never seen again.

Squadronaires and also of Glenn Miller who, sadly, was later killed in an air crash; British singers Anne Shelton and Vera Lynn also proved very popular.

The American Red Cross were very much in evidence. They had a centre not only at Burtonwood but all over the area, with two in Warrington alone. The centres provided a library, writing room, soft drinks and coffee but no tea! These refuges could be used by anyone wearing a military uniform.

One other aspect of Burtonwood which required an element of secrecy, even though this was very difficult to maintain, was the transport of aircraft from Liverpool docks to the airbase. Many aircraft arrived in pieces, packed in crates whilst some of the smaller types were transported whole but with their wings folded. There were plenty of official photographs taken, though, and these show just how busy the docks area and the surrounding streets of Liverpool were as the American war machine went into full swing.

One very under-recorded feature of the war in Cheshire was the brave work done by the ATA (Air Transport Auxiliary) pilots, many of them women. During the war there was not just an acute shortage of aircraft but also nowhere nearly enough pilots. Each pilot was required for combat and something needed to be done urgently to provide qualified people to deliver aircraft from the factory to an operational station. Both men and women were trained as Ferry Pilots but what was not fair at the beginning of the programme is that women were only paid two-thirds of the men's rate. Thanks to the direct intervention of Sir Stafford Cripps, equal pay was agreed but this was not adopted for other occupations during the war.

Each pilot was issued with a manual which gave operational information on how to fly all the aircraft produced during the war, of which there were many. The manual was divided into six sections containing trainers, single-engined fighters, twin-engined aircraft, medium-sized bombers, big four-engined bombers and also flying boats. The Ferry Pilots were busy all over the north-west including Woodford, Broughton and the Fairey factory near Stockport.

Ansons were used to relay the ATA pilots to the production sites and the workers there gradually got used to seeing young ladies at the controls of a huge bomber. The qualifications needed to train to become a pilot included being able to either drive a car or ride a horse. The minimum height was 5 ft 4 ins though the lasses were allowed to stand on tiptoe.

It was not just the RAF and aircraft factories which were busy in Cheshire, though, because the Fleet Air Arm, the navy and the shipbuilders were also busy fighting the Germans.

Chapter 5

Fighting at Sea

There has been an obvious and excusable focus on the part played in the war by the Liverpool side of the Mersey but, as is often the case, there are two sides to every story and so it is that there were also some very important and secret activities going on along the Wirral coastline, too. Apart from the Cammell Laird shipyard, there was a training base for naval personnel at Croft near Warrington and at Wallasey and Ellesmere Port, and trawlers were being converted to minesweepers and escort vessels.

Prior to the war it was realised that the estuary defences around Liverpool were just not good enough so three huge anti-aircraft towers were constructed at Bromborough. They looked like the massive oil platforms with which we are familiar today but these towers were a new concept at the time. Once the main construction was completed, the towers were towed into the river and secured to the seabed. The rigs were inter-connected by means of scaffolding with walkways and had anti-aircraft and machine guns mounted on them. These were designed to provide an aircraft deterrent and worked in conjunction with land-based batteries but they were probably more effective against submarines laying mines than protecting Liverpool from the Blitz.

It was obviously vital to protect the shipping approaches and, initially, the army had established two forts to protect the entrance to the Mersey. These were at Seaforth on the now long gone Lancashire (north) side of the river and Perch Rock at New Brighton on the Cheshire bank (south side). The latter is now a splendid museum containing lots of information relating to the Second World War.

The forts had been built in 1826 following the Napoleonic Wars; the solid stone walls were 32 ft high on the landward side and 40 ft high facing the sea. There is also a lighthouse in the area and this was used as an ROC observation post during the war.

Every possible protection had to be given to the Mersey approaches because the number of shipping movements in and out

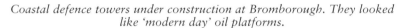

Coastal defence towers under construction at Bromborough. They looked like 'modern day' oil platforms.

Perch Rock at New Brighton guarded the entrance to the Atlantic and the Rock channel.

of the area was staggering. During the course of the war, 120 million tons of ocean-going shipping and an estimated 12,000 ships had to be docked, unloaded, repaired, victualled, re-armed, if necessary, and returned to the sea.

There were no containers in those days and huge numbers of dockers and support staff were kept hard at work. These people often had to operate under blackout conditions and be always prepared for an air raid. In addition to the ocean-going vessels, some 32 million tons of coastal traffic was also dealt with. Many of these movements, especially the destinations of armament shipments, had to be kept secret and processed by an army of clerks. The whole operation was comparable to the system of timetables which controlled the railways.

It is estimated, probably with some accuracy, that 4,700,000 troops passed through the port of Liverpool during hostilities. Among the varied cargo of food and armaments, aircraft on their way to Burtonwood and Warton, near Blackpool, also passed through. Later on in the war, four-engined bombers could be flown via Canada to the US bases but the fighters with less of a fuel range had to be transported by sea. Some were carried in huge holds but there were also lots of smaller vessels which meant that aircraft were carried on open decks. The wings, propellers and engines were packed in waterproof fabric but the fuselages were covered in cosmoline which was a sort of rubber-like cocoon which had to be scraped off at the US bases.

Obviously there were times when there was a shortage of berths and the ships were kept waiting in mid channel which meant that they were even more vulnerable to attack. One solution was to use two vessels each with a crane mounted on them which made unloading possible in mid channel. Ironically, these floating cranes had been built in Germany during the First World War and had been brought to Britain following the reparations which the Germans had to pay after losing the war. One monster was called *Mammoth* and the slightly smaller version was called *Samson*.

The main worry for the men who fought at sea was mines. At the beginning of the war, the German boffins were far ahead of their British equivalents in the development of magnetic mines. What the British needed was a stroke of luck and fortunately this was not long in coming.

A German bomber dropped two mines into the Thames estuary on an ebbing tide. These landed in soft mud and a very brave bomb disposal unit dismantled the mines. A way of neutralising them was then found which involved passing an electric cable around the hull of a ship which cancelled out its own magnetism. This method became known as degaussing, after the German scientist, Carl Friedrich Gauss, who specialized in the theories of electricity and magnetism. Ships composed largely of wood were obviously not so vulnerable to magnetic mines and this is why fishing trawlers were used as minesweepers but even they were more effective when they were degaussed.

At the very start of hostilities, trawlers mainly from Grimsby, Hull and Fleetwood were requisitioned and sent in great secret to workshops on the Wirral coast to be refitted and their crews given an all too brief training with regard to their wartime duties. Once again I am grateful for the clear memories of Joyce Openshaw,

> *When I was working in the cypher rooms in Liverpool, I looked at the Cheshire side of the Mersey to watch the trawlers doing their work. My father owned the Iago trawler fleet which operated out of Fleetwood and all of our best ships were pressed into war service as minesweepers.*

Trawler owner Lionel Marr also told me,

> *Our company had trawlers operating out of Fleetwood and Hull and, like all of us owners, we accepted that our most modern vessels were needed for active service and so were their crews. Each trawler was put under the command of a very young naval officer but all the lads knew who was the boss. You can't argue with a fishing boat skipper who has learned to cope with force 10 storms whilst still catching fish. It is no wonder that they were so good at locating mines and marking their position in order to have them blown up.*

Despite all these efforts, the convoys suffered heavy losses during the early years of the war as the wreck maps show very clearly. Obviously the loss of oil tankers was keenly felt especially if they were coming in fully loaded to refineries in the Stanlow area. The grave news of the sinking of the *El Oso*, which was mined on 17th January 1940, was kept secret but as 36 of her crew were from Merseyside and the Wirral area, news obviously leaked out.

Even the loss of an empty tanker was a disaster. The *Dosnia* left Stanlow heading for South Africa when she struck a mine on

26th October 1940 when she was in balance. She sank when twelve nautical miles off New Brighton. She had been built in Glasgow in 1938 and her fate, like others, was kept a close secret.

Apart from fuel being a vital commodity, of equal importance was food. The *Chagres* was a steamship mined and sunk 25 nautical miles off New Brighton on 9th February 1940 and was on passage from Nigeria carrying bananas which occasionally appeared on the menu of British restaurants. Edith Watson remembers,

> *My first sight of a banana was when I was five. We were in a British Restaurant in Chester and it consisted of black slices swimming in a thin custard. I was surprised to find out when I was about ten that, in fact, bananas were yellow and had to be skinned!*

Also vital during the war was raw cotton and silk. Even though many textile mills converted for use in the war effort as ration stores or munitions warehouses, some were still needed to produce civilian clothing and uniforms. Some of the silk mills around Macclesfield were also kept busy producing material for parachutes and some even produced tiny maps printed on thin silk material for use by secret agents in the field. These were folded and placed in cigarette lighters or in the hollow heels of shoes.

During the war, merchant seamen always had a legitimate grumble and nobody in their right mind could argue with them. At sea they faced the same risks – or arguably an even greater one – as the crews of the Royal Navy who were able to fight back. Also, as Edwin Davies recalls,

> *Once you hit a mine or a torpedo you knew that your wages stopped immediately and if you were killed your dependent got nowt. The survivors faced great hardship and your family would starve unless you could find another ship. It was bad enough facing the sea and the bloody Germans without always being worried about*

money. We also felt defenceless and we all wanted to fight back.

By 1940, some merchant ships were given Lewis guns and, later, the much more efficient Oerlikons were provided. Many good merchant seamen worked on the coastal vessels and Ron Morley told me,

> *I operated mostly out of Liverpool and Stanlow and my home was in New Brighton. We were told not to talk about what we were carrying but I have to admit that there was some loose talk when lads were ashore and had a skinful. My favourite pub was the Pilot Boat. This was where lads met when they had been sunk and they were looking for another berth. It was always hard to find your way through the censors to find out what ships had been sunk, what they had been carrying and which lads had been lost.*

Over time I have managed to track down a few of the coastal vessels which had been sunk. The steam coaster *Gorsethorn* which was built in Selby in 1917 was sunk 13 miles off New Brighton on 8th December 1940. She was on passage from Preston with a cargo of Lancashire coal to Ireland. The *Calcium* built at Greenock in 1918 was owned by ICI and was sunk 17 nautical miles off New Brighton on 30th December 1940. She was on her way to the limestone quarries of North Wales and she was in ballast. The *Penrhos* was even older and came from the Yarwood Company of Northwich in Cheshire in 1904. She was built a long way inland but her role was initially associated with the River Weaver. The Weaver is still often called the 'river of Salt' and these vessels once exported raw salt to British markets. On 1st January 1942 she was carrying limestone chippings when she struck a mine and sank 24 nautical miles from New Brighton. She was on passage from Penmaenmawr to Liverpool and was sunk close to the Great Orme headland and all her four crew were drowned.

The Pilot Boat was a popular pub for merchant seamen during the war.
They were told not to let the drink loosen their tongues!

Such losses in this area and all over the UK and beyond meant that the minesweepers were kept under constant pressure. In September 1939 and in great secrecy, the Admiralty, remembering the events of the First World War requisitioned trawlers, some of which were still under construction. In addition, during the war, a total of 83 trawlers were purpose-built to function as minesweepers and escort vessels. Morris Austin recalls,

I was ten when the war started and in view of my name I should have been a car spotter but this was not true in my case. Kids in the war did not think of danger as it was just part of normal life. Many of my friends were aircraft spotters and they spent lots of time on the high hills above Birkenhead but I was different. All my family had either been fishermen or ship builders and this explains how I became a wartime ship spotter. I had an old telescope and the local bobby and home guard lads realised that I was not the youngest spy in the world. I've got grandchildren now and they have pictures on their bedroom wall of Wayne Rooney, Stevie Gerrard and pop stars. For me it was wall-to-wall ships. I had one of the SS Celtic which reminds me of the heyday of the Transatlantic liner, many of which were built at Cammell Laird where my family worked. I also had a photograph of the troopship HMT Lancashire which was near as I could get to HMT Cheshire. My favourite has to be the Fleetwood trawler Kirkella and I have a photograph of her taken in 1945 as she was docked at Ellesmere Port. She was being converted back into a fishing vessel after working in the war as a minesweeper. One of my uncles was working on her and I was taken to see her. There were some small shipyards in this area and this has never been properly recognised. Do me a favour and do something to redress the balance.

Not only do events like this need to be recorded, but the brave deeds of the trawler crews also need to be written down. I spent some time with Alec Chumley who told me over a pint in the Pilot Boat pub not far from Perch Rock,

I was thought to be a bit weird by the rest of my family. Our men folk had all worked in the Crewe railway locomotive works since 1879 but I always wanted to go to sea. In 1939 I signed on as deckhand on a Fleetwood trawler. In 1940 after only one storm-tossed voyage, our ship was suddenly sent to Birkenhead and adapted to work as a minesweeper. This was kept secret and I was told to go home for a week which I did. All I know was that people were talking about a dynamo. It was only much later that I realised that this was the code name for the evacuation of Dunkirk. There was a young and spotty naval officer officially in charge but we all knew who was

The trawler, Kirkella, *which served as a minesweeper during the war. The wooden hulls of trawlers were better able to cope with the anti-magnetic mines.*

*boss and that was our skipper. On 26 May 1940 we were
in the thick of the action with bombs, shells and bullets
flying everywhere. I was either too scared or too busy
getting brave lads on board to realise that I was in danger
but the old trawler men were brilliant. Nobody panicked
and the old hands looked after us young 'uns and they did
that all through the war when we swept mines. It was good
to get home and after the war I worked as a fitter in
Cammell Laird until I retired in 1978.*

Most people who worked at Cammell Laird during the war
realised the importance of their work and its importance to the
war effort. Eric Postlethwaite who was a retired schoolmaster
when I spoke to him in Birkenhead in 2007 smiled as he told me,

*I remember my 14th birthday in August 1940 when I was
living just a stone's throw from Cammell Laird where my
dad worked in the drawing office. Everybody was working
hammer and tongs as warships were being built and the
luxurious liners were being converted into troop ships.
Even my great grandfather had worked in this yard and
you can see why I have iron in my blood and why I later
taught metalwork. For my birthday I got what I asked for
which was a painting and a model of a ship called the*
Birkenhead *which was built in 1846. My relatives worked
on her. From that day I began to collect as many things,
especially photographs, as I could relating to Cammell
Laird.*

During our chat I realised that Eric had a particular affection for
two ships: the *Mauritania* and the *Ark Royal*. The *Mauritania*
launched on 28th July 1938, was 772 ft long 89 ft wide, and was
fitted with 42,000 hp engines, weighed 35,739 tons and had a
speed of 23 knots. Her maiden voyage to New York was on 17th
June 1939 and she must have been a splendid sight. This pristine
condition did not last long and in August 1939 she returned to

Cammell Laird to be converted into a troop ship. During hostilities she carried around 35,000 troops and travelled 540,000 miles. On September 1946 she returned to her home yard to be refitted as a cruise liner and she was in service until 1965 having had a proud history.

The *Ark Royal* also came off the stocks in 1938 and was at that time the finest aircraft carrier in the world. There was an element of humour relating to the launch of the vessel. Lady Maud Hoare had the privilege of breaking the champagne over the vessel; she swung the bottle twice but failed to break it. Voices from the workers were heard to shout 'Give it to Dixie' referring to Dean, the famous Everton centre forward. Another much ruder call was 'Hoares are only good for one job'.

During the war, Cammell Laird vessels did sterling service and some sadly did not survive; during the war itself the yard

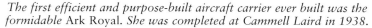

The first efficient and purpose-built aircraft carrier ever built was the formidable Ark Royal. *She was completed at Cammell Laird in 1938.*

produced 106 fighting ships. The *Ark Royal* survived the conflict despite the fact that Lord Haw Haw reported that she had been sunk four times. When it was reported that the *Bismarck* had been sunk partly because of Swordfish flown from *Ark Royal* we can see a real Cheshire connection. The carrier was built in Birkenhead and the Swordfish were assembled near Stockport.

Another Laird vessel has become immortal in the history of naval warfare. This was the battleship *Prince of Wales*. It was in the wardroom of this vessel that Prime Minister Winston Churchill met with President Roosevelt and signed the Atlantic Charter.

I have a personal memory of another of Birkenhead's vessels, this time relating to the submarine *Thetis*. I had relatives who worked on submarines at Vickers in Barrow and at Cammell Laird at Birkenhead. I clearly remember an event in 1943 when I was seven. One of my school friends was collected by his mother who had to tell him that his father had been killed in the submarine HMS *Thunderbolt*. The vessel had been operating off the coast of Sicily and had sunk two submarines and five support vessels. Then she was sunk herself by depth charges with the loss of all 63 men on board.

It was only in 2001 when I began to research this present book that I realised that the *Thunderbolt* had been sunk not once but twice! On the first occasion she had been called HMS *Thetis*.

With the clouds of war gathering, Britain needed to update her submarine fleet, as well as increasing the number of vessels in active operation. The *Thetis* was the first of the new Triton class submarines and was 240 ft long and had a displacement of 1,029 tons. She was launched on July 1st 1939 and then set off for her diving trials. In addition to her trials crew of around 50, there were also a couple of caterers, a Mersey pilot and an unknown number of shipyard officials on board. Just off Llandudno she dived but soon began to flood and could not be refloated, and settled on the bottom some 40 metres (130 ft) down. A few people escaped using the new Davis escape apparatus but more than 60 people lost their lives. The reasons for the tragedy have been

The launch of the Thetis. *She was sunk not once, but twice, and was also called the* Thunderbolt.

difficult to unravel but it would seem that too many people were on board, and that human error was involved.

There did not seem to have been any major design faults and so it was decided that the expensive vessel should be salvaged and her name changed and sent into battle under the name of *Thunderbolt*.

Jeff Banks remembered the *Thunderbolt* because his father-in-law worked on her. He also recalled that,

> *As a lad of ten I watched all sorts of activities going on around New Brighton and I remember seeing what is now called the Merchant Ship Fighter Unit. This involved launching Hurricane fighters by means of rockets from the deck of a small ship. I saw this being tested but obviously I didn't realise what was going on at the time because it was so secret.*

The way this worked was actually cost effective despite what has often been suggested. When a German aircraft was sighted, usually a Focke-Wulf Condor, the Hurricane fighter, which did not have the range to be launched from land, was rocketed into action. Its speed and fire power soon knocked out the enemy and then the fighter plane was ditched in the sea and the pilot rescued. The cost of the Hurricane had to be balanced against the saving of a ship and the loss of the German aircraft. The Germans lost a crew of four whilst the British pilot was saved. It has to be said that the protection of the convoys had to be the first priority because not only did Britain need to import and export weapons but it also had to be fed.

Chapter 6

The Struggle for Food

There is no doubt that the disruption to food supplies during the war affected everyone as the age of the horse was superseded by the internal combustion engine. For some time, though, the two systems ran very much in parallel. Ivy Yates of Meols, on the Wirral, fondly recalled the days of the horse,

As the war started, I remember the ice-cream man coming round the streets with his horse and cart, swinging a big wooden rattle to attract attention. Then there was the milk float, also pulled by a horse with big churns strapped to either side of its back. The driver, often a local farmer, used to dip measures into the churns or use a tap and customers brought their own jugs. I remember my grandmother carrying her gill measure under a blanket and going to the pub to collect her supply of the demon drink. At that time only men went to pubs which to say the least were basic. There was sand and sawdust on the floor and the spittoons were often full. There was smoke everywhere. How things have changed and thank goodness for that. The local fish and chip shop always did good business, especially during the war. We used to carry ours in an earthenware jar to save on the paper. Fish was never rationed and some trawler men were still risking the sea and the Germans to earn a living. In those days fish could not be stored because nobody had fridges. These earthenware pots easily held a pennyworth of fish and for half this price you got a load of chips. Our earthenware pots were used daily and in those days women were better cooks than the lasses are today, and we made use of the cheapest cuts of meat. Tatie pies in them days were smashing!

Bill Motson remembers when the tractor began to take over the work of horses in the fields,

'All my family were farm workers and had worked all over Shropshire, North Wales and Cheshire. We all loved our 'osses. I were just a lad in 1940 when we began to see steam-powered tractors arriving. Some were made by Fodens where my grandfather worked. My dad said that tractors would never replace the 'osses because these bloody monsters could not produce the manure which we spread on our fields.

The country was hard pressed to produce enough food because many young men had been drafted into the forces. This labour vacuum had to be filled and the answer was obvious – women. Many girls volunteered and some were conscripted into the Women's Land Army. This organisation had been set up in 1917 but was disbanded as soon as that war was over which was very

Even some of the older Foden steam tractors were brought into service during the war.

short-sighted. Britain then returned to a situation where we imported most of our food, including eggs from the continent. As war became obvious and everybody knew that supply lines would be disrupted, the Women's Land Army was reformed and

Cattle grazing the rich land surrounding the Burtonwood airbase in the summer of 1944.

organised on a regional basis. In Cheshire, the Army chair-person was Mrs Ernest Johnson of Heys and her telephone number was Heyes 209. The secretary was Miss E. L. Manley whose office was located on Northgate Street in Chester and her telephone number was Chester 447. These numbers indicate just how few telephones were available at that time.

Looked at in retrospect, it would seem that the Land Army was put into operation swiftly and easily but this was not true and a mountain of paperwork was generated. It is no wonder that paper was soon in short supply. Winnie Marchant told me,

> *I was nearly 18 when the war started. I had worked in the silk mills in Macclesfield from the age of 15 and the work was hard, the hours were long and it was boring. I only*

One of the many Government posters urging people to avoid wasting food.

knew what fresh air was when we went for a walk in the park and I didn't know one end of a cow from another but I did know they could give you a painful kick. Anyhow, in 1941 I decided to join the Land Army. I can still remember the name of the lady who signed my acceptance form. She was called Miss Manley and, along with her letter, I was given two lists. One gave details of the uniform I was to be given free of charge and the other gave a list of the minimum civilian clothes which I was advised to pack. We were all told not to forget our identity cards, national insurance details and our ration books. I also took my Post Office Savings Bond form. I had saved up £5 and had bought some defence bonds with a 3% interest rate as I thought it was my way of helping with the war effort. I was given a third class railway warrant to the nearest railway station to where we were to be working. I was welcomed because I had my own bike and was told to take that with me.

The Land Army Uniform

Twelve items were provided free of charge:

1. A rainproof mackintosh
2. A khaki overall coat
3. Two fawn shirts with a turn-down collar
4. A pair of corduroy breeches
5. A pair of dungarees
6. A green knitted pullover
7. Three pairs of fawn stockings
8. A pair of heavy brown shoes
9. A pair of rubber gum boots
10. A brown felt hat
11. A green arm band with a crown on it
12. A button hole badge which could be worn with civilian clothes

There were Land Army training centres in all counties but most girls were trained on the spot by local farmers. Most, but not all, farmers were both pleasant and welcoming but the local Land Army office had an eagle-eyed inspector who looked after the welfare of the land lasses as they were often called in Cheshire.

The Army had its very own magazine which was published monthly and cost three pence and could be delivered by post. It was called *Land Girl* and there was also a comprehensive manual of the same name, written by Shewell Cooper, packed full of useful information. Audrey Pearson now living in Doncaster remembers working near Neston,

Although the work was hard, I was never fitter in my life. We got 32 shillings for a 48-hour week and if we worked overtime we got eight pence an hour extra. If we were fed on the farm we got only 16 shillings but the food was usually so good that we all thought it was worth it. I was never ill but it was good to know that we had sick pay which none of us had been used to before the days of the Health Service.

Wilfred Barnes looked at the Land Girls from the other side of the fence. He remembered,

The girls arriving at my dad's farm near Congleton were brought into Cheshire for basic training and there's nowt like training on the job. We always had to fight to produce good food and, long before the war was over, some of the lasses were as good a fighter as any of the men and were a bloody sight better looking. I should know 'cos I married one of 'em and my brother married another.

There is no doubt that the Land Army did a good job and helped to feed the country and supplement the imported rations. The 'Dig for Victory' campaign also worked well. Many people over the

Just three of the many posters printed, exhorting people to grow their own food.

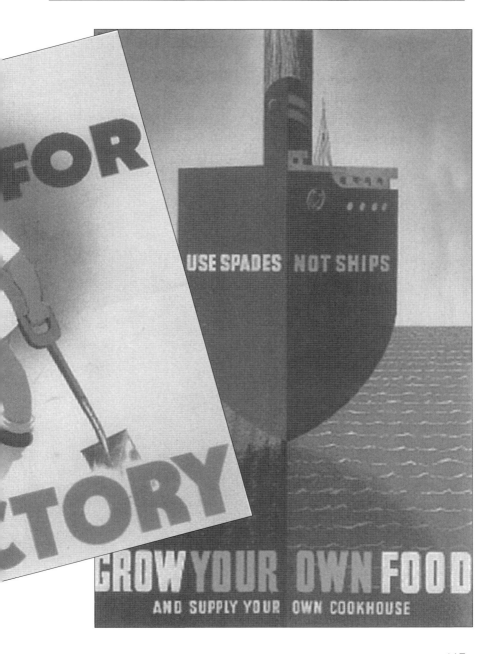

years had loved working on their allotments or in their gardens; there was always a 'green' community spirit before the war but these bonds were substantially strengthened during hostilities. The emphasis, though, was on growing vegetables rather than flowers, and in the case of the larger plots, land was given over to keeping chickens, rabbits and, occasionally, a pig. Several of the county's parks, like Queen's Park in Crewe also set aside plots for growing food. Even the flower beds at railway stations were dug over and replaced by vegetable patches.

Old stoves were fired back into life to be used in garden huts and even dilapidated lean-to sheds. Alan Backhouse had a plot quite close to the Risley Ordnance Factory and he told me,

We got my granddad's old stove working and burned old fence posts and plant cuttings. We put it into a greenhouse and even during the terrible winters of 1940 and 1941 we managed to keep our grapevine alive and we also grew tomatoes and a few flowers to keep the ladies happy.

Many schools had their own playing fields and these were converted into gardens and the children copied the posters of colourful cartoon characters which were published. Potatoes were a really popular item and most children could sing,

Potato Pete
Here's the man who ploughs the field
Here's the girl who lifts up the yield
Here's the man who deals with the clamp
So that millions of jaws can chew and champ
That's the story and here's the star
Potato Pete! Eat up Eat up
Ta Ta! Ta Ta!

This ditty soon became famous and it was set to music and sung by Betty Driver who later became famous in TV's *Coronation Street*.

George Pemberton, who was ten when the war started and who went on to work as a carpenter at Cammell Laird, recalls helping his mum with cooking and weighing out the rations.

Stella Fagan had a similar tale to tell,

We lived near West Kirby on the Wirral. During the war, my mother taught me to cook and make the best use of the cheaper cuts of meat. When I grew up, I earned my living as a cook before retiring on my 70th birthday in 2006.

Despite the efforts of the Land Army and the 'Dig For Victory' campaign, rationing was vital and looked at in today's context the quantities allowed were minimal, to say the least. I recently gave a lecture about home life in the Second World War and I pre-warned the audience to bring with them their most recent shopping list but without telling them why. At the start of my talk, I unwrapped what was the weekly ration for one person for one week during the war. This consisted of two ounces of sugar, four of butter, two of cooking fat, four of bacon, two of tea, two of cheese, two of flour, two lamb chops and one egg. The meat was not calculated by weight but by price. The cheaper the cut the more meat you got which was why housewives of this period were both good and economical cooks. Over the period of the war the ration allowances per week did vary according to what was available as this table indicates:

Item	Maximum	Minimum
Bacon (or ham)	8 oz	4 oz
Sugar	16 oz	8 oz
Loose tea	4 oz	2 oz
Cheese	8 oz	1 oz
Butter	8 oz	2 oz
Lard	3 oz	2 oz
Margarine	12 oz	4 oz
Egg	one	one
Milk	3 pints	3 pints

Rationing obviously affected every person in Britain and thousands of people – often women – were involved in printing, processing and distributing ration books. What the authorities did want to keep as secret as possible was when the allowances were reduced; they did not wish to publicise that the Germans were being successful in disrupting the supply lines. The Ministry of Food were constantly busy producing advice to make the maximum use of the rations. With reference to tea, the Ministry of Food Bulletin No 3, dated June 1940, commented, 'We should all use less tea and if each person gave up one spoonful, we should have room for 50,000 tons of war material in one year.' One has to remember that there were no tea bags until the early 1950s. Alice Repton recalls,

We never had to worry about tea because my mother worked in the NAAFI at the RAF station in West Kirkby. She was as honest as the day is long and as she was washing up, she was allowed to strain off the leaves from the huge teapots. She then brought the leaves home, dried them in the oven and re-used them. My dad worked at Cammell Laird's shipyard and he loved his tea even more than he loved his beer.

There was also advice on how to make the best use of butter. There was no pre-packaging and instead it arrived in barrels and was cut, weighed and patted into shape. People were told to eat their bread with the butter side down so that it made contact with the taste buds on the tongue.

There was also a suggestion to ration water, and for water wardens to enforce it. Amanda Dowling remembers her grandmother, who was 81 in 1940,

She had a tin bath hung up in the washhouse and took it in front of the fire and filled it with hot water from kettles. 'No bugger is using a ruler to measure my watter', she grinned.

One aspect which was kept very secret during the war concerned the subject of looting. This rare photograph shows a soldier guarding rations salvaged from a shop following an air raid on Birkenhead.

Petrol was rationed from 16th September 1939. This did not affect too many people as few had cars in those days. The standard type of petrol was replaced by a lower quality mixture called Pool. Commercial diesel and petrol was stained red – and still is to this day – to prevent misuse of the system. For a 20 hp vehicle the allowance was four gallons per month and less for smaller vehicles. WVS ladies and other voluntary workers were given sufficient fuel to enable them to carry out their work. The only sign of relaxation was that double rations were allowed over the Christmas holiday which was very welcome. Otherwise rations had to be used by the week and could not be saved up – if you failed to collect your ration you lost it.

Over Christmas, people baked cakes shaped like Anderson shelters, Spitfires and tanks, and they used carrots as a substitute for sugar in their recipes. Audrey Simpson who lived near Chester remembers,

We used grated carrots, suet and some pre-war sultanas and nutmeg which we had saved up and kept in an airtight tin to stuff our Christmas chicken. Our meagre sweet ration was saved up for weeks and wrapped up in small packets and hung on a tiny tree. We were all told to buy a small tree and to keep it properly planted ready for next year and we enjoyed keeping it alive. This saved valuable timber for the war effort.

Clothing ration books were also introduced which could also be used for household textiles such as bedding and towels. People were give extra coupons that they could use for work clothes, such as overalls. Toys were always in short supply and most had to be spruced up and recycled. Stan Mitchell of Wallasey was a great make do and mender,

Just before the war I worked over the river in Liverpool at the Meccano works. During the war we made Sten guns but I had a few pieces of loose bits which I gave to my two lads who made model cranes with them.

1942-43 CLOTHING BOOK

This book may not be used until the holder's name, full postal
address and National Registration (Identity Card) Number
have been plainly written below IN INK.

NAME .... *R. G. HYDE* ....
(BLOCK LETTERS)

ADDRESS .... *12 HYLTON AVENUE,* ....
(BLOCK LETTERS)

(TOWN) .... *WALLASEY* .... (COUNTY) .... *Cheshire*

NATIONAL REGISTRATION (IDENTITY CARD) NUMBER

LDCQ / 302 / 2

Read the instructions within carefully, and take great care not to lose this book
Page 1

Clothes rationing finally ended in March 1949.

The majority of people managed very well on their rations and
for some there were added bonuses. Some of the larger factories
where workers were required for overtime had restaurants and
often had visits from the BBC *Workers' Playtime* artists. Most of
the large towns and a few of the smaller ones had British
Restaurants which soon became much loved institutions. They
were set up by the Ministry of Food and run by local communities
on a non-profit-making basis. They were intended to ease the
pressure on the rations and ensured that everyone could find
something to eat. Initially they were called Community Kitchens
but Winston Churchill insisted that the name was changed to
British Restaurants. Some of the smaller places did not qualify to
be a fully-fledged restaurant and were called 'Cash and Carry
outlets'. The food available at these outlets was delivered from a
main restaurant. Meals cost a maximum of nine pence; nobody

could have more than one helping and the quantities served were carefully measured.

Apart from these static food outlets, there were also mobile canteens operated by the Women's Voluntary Service (WVS) where meals never cost more than one shilling and six pence. The Salvation Army also manned some mobile canteens for the use of the many servicemen and women around Chester, Warrington and Merseyside. There was an impressive array of British Restaurants in Chester, including the Campbell Memorial Hall at Broughton and the Mission at Westminster Hall but arguably the most impressive seems to have been the outlet on Upper Northgate Street. There were also cash and carry outlets in Francis Street and on Cliveden Road.

With the combination of rations, 'Growing your own', 'Digging for Victory', the Land Army and factory canteens, Britain could work hard, keep busy and break all records.

Chapter 7

Factories and Logistics

For the huge factories to work at full capacity, it was essential to maintain an efficient transport system which could bring in the raw materials and then deliver the finished products to where they were needed. Nowhere was this logistical system more vital than in the chemical industry which produced vast amounts of explosives. It was in this field that Cheshire scientists were world leaders.

In 1860 the Alkali complex of John Hutchison and Company had built a set of offices from which to run what became the largest chemical factory in the world. For nearly 10 years John Brunner and Ludwig Mond worked for the Hutchison Company. In 1872, however, the gifted pair left in order to set up their own company and pioneered the Solway Ammonia Process. Their first factory was set up at Winnington, near Northwich. Brunner and Mond bought the estate from the Warrington family and from 1873 the partners and their families lived there whilst they built up their chemical complex within the estate. By 1820 the main house had been extensively redeveloped and extended. The

Brunner-Mond-ICI Company still employ Cheshire workers to this day.

Secret work was carried out in this plant during the war. Fawcett and Gibson, two very talented chemists had developed a thermoplastic polymer called 'Polythene'. During the war variants of this substance were evolved and used as insulators, especially for the new radar equipment. These secrets seem to have been kept from the prying eyes of the Germans but were then given to the Americans as part of what was termed the 'Lend-Lease' scheme. It was therefore the American companies which made vast fortunes from the production of polythene much to the annoyance of the Cheshire-based chemists.

I had a long conversation in 1998 with Ben Watson who worked as a driver in the salt rich areas of Cheshire. He told me,

Obviously in the war we didn't know what was being produced once we had delivered the raw salt. I drove from the mines to Brunner Monds in Winnington and to the glassworks at Pilkington's in St Helens. Driving was not easy in those days because many journeys were done at night during the black out and the roads could be a bit bumpy.

Glass was vital to the war effort and at Pilkington's there were lots of secret inventions taking place, as well as the production of 'normal' glass which was needed to repair bomb damage. Bullet-proof glass, searchlights, portholes, periscopes and other very sophisticated equipment had to be produced at great speed.

There were also many other uses for salt-based products. Chlorine was the deadly gas used in the First World War but thankfully neither side used it in the 1939–45 war, no doubt fearing a massive retaliation. Nevertheless, gas masks were produced in their millions and huge stocks of chlorine produced. Chlorine was also necessary, of course, for the bleaching of paper and textiles. At the same time, chemists were hard at work producing other deadly chemicals.

Carbon tetrachloride is another dangerous chemical used in the production of chloroform, explosives, paints, plastics, glass and the chemical DDT (dichlorodiphenyltrichloroethane). Salt is chemically known as sodium chloride and sodium itself is a metal which melts at 98°C. It was used in the production of antiknock, a substance added to petrol to increase its octane rating, especially at a time when the quality of the fuel was being scaled down.

Sodium hydroxide is a basic material used in the production of both washing soda and soap. In view of the demands made on raw materials in the war, soap products were soon rationed. Four coupons were allowed per month. Each of the following carried one coupon so a choice had to be made between 4 ounces of hard soap, 3 ounces of toilet soap or 6 ounces of soap powder.

All the pressure on the transport system meant that the production of vehicles had to be given a high priority. The family firm of Foden based in Sandbach began building steam-powered tractors as early as 1868; their last steam-powered truck only left the assembly line in 1934 and many were still in operation at the start of the war. By 1931 Foden were also making flat-bed diesel lorries and these only went out of production in the 1960s as articulated vehicles were evolving. In the 1930s Edwin Richard Foden left the family business to set up his own company, ERF. Both companies relied heavily on the engines produced by Gardner, whose factory had been established on Duke Street in Manchester. Gardner's main business involved the production of marine engines, but the company had also successfully modified the design to power road vehicles. Gardner were in operation from the 1860s well into the 1990s.

Mel Harper remembers the Foden factory in the 1940s,

We were making tractors and flat beds. My job was to fit the engines into position and we knew that the Gardner engines were thirsty buggers but their designers were hard at work to improve this aspect. We all knew fine-tuning of each engine was essential and the blokes who assembled the bodies were equally keen to attend to every detail.

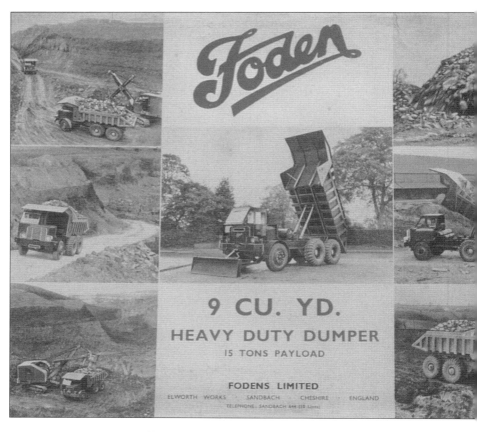

A publicity shot for Foden dump trucks.

The main rival to both Foden and ERF was Leyland Motors based in Chorley, Lancashire. (There is now a Commercial Vehicles Museum at Leyland and in this there are a number of vintage ERF and Foden vehicles.) During the war, Foden and ERF turned out many army vehicles and fire engines. Foden continued in full production until well into the 1980s.

Many people think that the Rolls-Royce-Bentley Motor Works at Crewe was only initiated in 1946. All this proves that the blanket of secrecy imposed during the war, even though quite thin at times, did actually work. The Rolls Royce Merlin engine was so successful that demand soon began to outstrip supply and secret so-called shadow factories were set up. Their function was to ensure that one or even two enemy bombing raids would not totally halt production. A Merlin factory was quietly built at Crewe in 1939 and we now know how successful and versatile this engine was. Wilf Ellison, my uncle, told me,

I served my apprenticeship at Rolls Royce in the 1920s. I was working on the Merlin engine in Derby in 1938 and it really was a beauty. It ran as smooth as silk, with hardly any vibration. In 1939 we were told that shadow factories were going to be built and that people there had to learn to assemble them but had no real training. Some of us were sent to help the new people and I was sent to Crewe.

The Merlin power plant also proved to be adaptable and was fitted to Spitfires, Hurricanes, the mighty Lancaster and many other aircraft. All the aeroplane engines were fitted with super chargers but at Crewe some Merlins were produced without this system. These engines were called Meteors and they were used to power first the Cromwell and later the Centurion tanks which saw action especially in the follow up to D-Day. My former university professor was John Cloudsley-Thompson who was a tank commander at this time and he told me,

To be honest none of our tanks could match the German Panzers on a one-to-one basis. The armament and body armour was not as good as theirs but the engines were bloody good and enabled many of us to get out of tricky situations.

Unlike many shadow factories, the Crewe works was not shut

down after the end of the war and, from 1947 onwards, Bentleys rolled off the Rolls Royce assembly line and now the company is German-owned!

It was not just the road system and the vehicles which drove along them which was a vital cog in the wartime struggle. It is impossible to underrate the role played by the railways at this time and again Crewe was one of the most important production sites. The link between northern Britain and the southern ports could not be broken if the war was to be won. There were two main routes: the East Coast route from Edinburgh to London via York and Doncaster and the West Coast route from Glasgow to London via Carnforth and Crewe. At Crewe there was a huge steam locomotive factory and extensive marshalling yards, all of which the Germans were well aware of.

These days the Settle–Carlisle Railway is regarded as more of a tourist attraction, but it was vitally important during the war. It provided a link between the East and West Coast routes and if either of these main lines had been successfully bombed then there was a ready-made diversion. Bill Donley worked as a signalman on the Settle–Carlisle line during the war. He recalled,

> *From 1939 onwards we ceased to regard ourselves as employed by one of the rival companies, instead we worked together to keep supplies running. I have never seen so many locomotive types. How some of those engines pulled such loads I will never know. The winters of 1940 and 1941 were a real trial and I felt guilty as I sat in my warm signal box and looked out to see so many men digging snow to keep this exposed line open.*

At the start of the war, Britain's railway network was already showing worrying signs of age and, by the 1930s, most of the locomotives, rolling stock and track were in need of replacement, and also a thorough overhaul. When war came, it was a race against time to keep everything moving. Apart from the hardware and the crews, a real pressure was placed upon the clerical and signalling staff who had to log each journey. Every movement was given a code number which was made up of a combination of letters and numbers. Even the crews themselves did not know where they were going or what they were carrying until they reported for duty.

All public transport, including train carriages, had their windows criss-crossed with sticky tape. This was called scrim and designed to reduce the number of splinters of glass that might result from an explosion. Rail crews in those days did not have any direct communication with their base apart from slowing down at signal boxes and the stringent blackout restrictions did not help. In the event of an air raid there was a very rudimentary system in operation involving large coloured boards. Green meant 'go', Orange meant 'enemy in the area' whilst Red meant that the enemy was ahead so the engine was stopped and the crew told to find the nearest cover.

The Germans obviously made strenuous efforts to disrupt the docks and the transport systems leading to and from them. The British government were well aware of this and of special importance was the supply of fuel oil. This put extra pressure on steam power and the coal mines were kept working at maximum capacity. The shortage of manpower meant that one in ten men called up were drafted into the mines. They were called Bevin Boys after Ernest Bevin, the Minister in charge. The Bevin Boys were recruited by ballot and there was no escape from this essential job.

All those who worked the locomotives knew just how vital coal was and soon had to learn to operate old and often unreliable and underpowered engines. A shortage of men meant that some were brought out of retirement and lads, some as young as sixteen, were also pressed into service. Firemen were promoted to become drivers and many of those previously employed as cleaners were literally elevated to the footplate. This shortfall of labour on the railways, as in many other places, was partly solved by employing women.

During the war, many maintenance procedures just had to be

Heavy vehicles such as tanks were moved around the country by train. The strain on the system was almost – but not quite – brought to breaking point.

ignored and, consequently, locomotives and rolling stock did break down through sheer wear and tear. The worst thing that could happen to a footplate crew was if the pressure gauge blew up because it showered glass and boiling water into the cab. Most, and probably all, locomotives had to pull loads in excess of their specification and this caused problems, especially in hilly areas. Older engines called bankers were placed close to known problem areas and were attached to the end of the trains to give them the extra power they needed to negotiate the inclines.

All the crews were aware that their loads were not to be discussed, and the general public were advised not to travel unless it was necessary. There were posters published and displayed everywhere emphasising this message. The footplate men took a more than careful look at the signs on the goods wagons and did not welcome the large letters M.D. They knew at this point that explosives were being delivered to the War Department.

It was not just the engines and the loads that could cause problems for the footplate crews. As much as six tons of coal might have to be shovelled into the firebox in the course of one shift so a fireman had to be fit. He also had to have a good aim to ensure that the coal was dropped in the right place in order to produce the correct temperature. If the area in the firebox was white, then coal had to be added but if it was red, then the fire was producing the right amount of steam and the fireman could enjoy a brief rest.

The fireman also often had the problem of a bunker of poor-quality coal, full of dust, which meant a low temperature was produced as it burned. Jeff Palmer, a fireman during the war, told me, *Some of the coal was of such poor quality that even Old Nick would not have used it in Hell.*

There were times when the crews had to be part of what they referred to as 'ghost trains'. This meant that among the passengers were some VIPs so extra censorship was necessary and security officers would be in evidence everywhere along the whole train. Apart from red tape, inferior coal, old engines, the carrying of bombs and also the threat of being bombed, the greatest

Willing ladies loading petrol tanks onto railway wagons. The amount of work done by women during the war was inestimable.

discomfort was caused by the blackout. At that time, most cabs were open to the elements and the firebox when opened could be easily seen from the air. The only solution was to cover the cab with a strong, black tarpaulin which meant that although it was now protected from the weather, the fumes and dust from the coal was concentrated in a confined space and, combined with the heat, especially in the summer, it could be suffocating.

By 8th May 1945, more than 400 train crew men had been killed and over 2,000 seriously wounded; these figures were kept secret until 1947. Unexploded bombs were another real hazard and all that could be done was to pass the area slowly, but it obviously put extra pressure on all those aboard who were aware of the situation. During the war, as many as 1.5 million train journeys were made and the demand for the production of new locomotives, as well as repairing old ones, was at times almost impossible to meet but, thankfully, not quite. Nowhere was this pressure more intense than in and around the Crewe locomotive works.

The Crewe factory had been built in 1840 by the Grand Junction Railway Company and the first steam locomotive came off the assembly line in 1843. Then followed what has been described as 'railway mania'. There were numerous company mergers prior to the First World Way but by 1923 the system was organised into four regions namely the London and North Eastern (LNER) the Southern (SR), the Great Western (GWR) and the London, Midland and Scottish (LMS). Each company produced its own locomotive works and there was great competition between them. The LMS works was at Crewe and had its own brick works, iron foundries, railway line factories and rolling stock production areas.

In the 1920s, however, there were worrying problems with the locomotives which seem to have been seriously underpowered. A talented team of engineers led by William Stanier reacted by designing some mighty machines. These were divided into classes of steam engines which were much loved by train spotters, and included such locomotives as the Princesses, Duchesses, Jubilees and especially the magnificent Black Fives. These engines were all made of high-quality steel and proved to be long-lasting after performing brilliantly in the war.

I met with several people who worked in the Crewe works during the war, including Bill Bowes who remembers working on the assembly line during the winter of 1941,

> *Snow often blasted into the shed and by the time the white flakes reached the floor they were black. I suppose you could say that once you were a skilled engineer you could adapt to any job and some of my mates were employed in other sheds and involved in assembling Covenanter tanks. I always preferred the Black Fives but we all knew how valuable these tanks were and 1,771 of this type were produced here in Crewe but also at Leyland Motors and the English Electric Works in Preston.*

The Covenanter, however, soon proved to be no match for the German Panzers and neither its superstructure nor its armaments were powerful enough and the cooling system was not efficient when moving at speed. My university professor was John Cloudsley Thompson who served as a tank commander in the

North African desert and later during the advance from the Normandy D-Day beaches. He told me,

We knew as early as 1943 that the Covenanter and other types were obsolete in battle but they really were excellent when they were adapted as bridge-laying vehicles and the Royal Engineers loved them.

All those who worked on the locomotives and the tanks at Crewe were told to keep their cards close to their chests and the failure of the Covenanters to deal with the Panzers and their poor cooling system was never revealed until well after the war although the tank crews were well aware of the problem.

It is no surprise to find that so much train spotting went on in and around Crewe and this was allowed to continue during the war as Maud Crompton recalls,

I was most unusual because I was a girl and most of the spotters were boys. I only started to go to Crewe station because I had to keep an eye on my young brother. At first we were not allowed access to the platforms but later we were tolerated but there was to be no cameras and we were all looked at carefully. Gradually things eased but I expect that most sensitive loads were transported at night. I remember early in 1945 when American troops passed through the station and they threw packets of sweets and chocolate to us. Sometimes fights broke out among those picking up the goodies. They also threw out empty fag packets, as they knew many kids collected them. I still remember seeing Lucky Strike cigarettes flying through the air!

Long before the start of the war, the canal system was regarded as obsolete but part of an impressive network known as the Cheshire Ring still carried some traffic and did link inland

The railway works at Crewe. This was one of the largest of its type in the world and the Black Five engines produced during the war were real workhorses.

factories to the sea. It obviously made sense to make use of this form of transport during the war.

The Ellesmere Canal, built between 1791 and 1795, was engineered by Thomas Telford and eventually had links to several canals, including the Shropshire Union. A vital junction was built at Ellesmere which eventually had the name 'Port' added to its title. Both the canal and the port were important during the war. There were flour mills which were vital for the production of bread and there was also a corrugated iron factory where Anderson shelters were produced, together with other essential pieces of equipment.

Canal traffic was obviously slow but it was very economical on fuel and capable of moving heavy goods, including coal and vehicles. The powered barges were called 'butty' boats or 'pudding' boats because of the shape of their cargo when loaded. There were problems with ice especially in the winters of 1940 and 1941, and weeds were also a problem in summer. The canal companies soon learned to deal with these problems and specially-built icebreakers and weed cutters were put into operation when needed, as Janice Green remembers,

My dad worked on the Shroppie (the Shropshire Union) all of his life. He was trained to deal with damaged or rotten lock gates but in winter he was on call to work on the icebreaker. This had a sharp metal front and was built so that it could be rocked from side to side and the men also had long-handled axes and specially adapted crowbars. It was a cold job but they did have a little cabin with a stove in it.

Vera Tyson had an uncle who worked on the Anderton Lift and she told me of its history and its use in the war,

Uncle Stan knew that, in the 1930s, German 'tourists' had paid visits to the lift and he was sure that it would be bombed. It was opened in 1874 and provided a 50-ft link

*Working to keep the canals open – weed clearing (above)
and ice-breaking (below)*

The Anderton Boat Lift now restored to its former glory.

between the Trent and Mersey Canal and the River Weaver where there were lots of vital electrical industries. It meant that cargoes could be moved from one waterway to the other without having to be loaded and unloaded using man and horsepower. At first it was operated by hydraulic power but in 1908 it was replaced by electricity. During 1941 and 1942 the old iron hydraulic system was removed and melted down for the war effort. There was no doubt that at this time it was vitally important and we were all sad when the lift was closed down in 1983.

There was no doubt that at that time the lift was in a dangerous condition due to corrosion but recently it has been renovated and is an important tourist attraction. Its history is a long and distinguished one and the Anderton Boat Lift is one of the wonders of the Canal Age.

Chapter 8

Keeping Up Morale

When war did finally erupt on 3rd/4th September 1939, the Government reacted by closing down entertainment venues. All radio stations, except the BBC Home Service, were taken off the air. This was very short-sighted because keeping up morale was absolutely essential and the country needed some outlet for leisure such as a visit to the theatre, cinema or sports venue. Also, many people had radio sets and if they couldn't listen to home broadcasts, they could instead tune into overseas stations, including Radio Hamburg which featured Lord Haw Haw who broadcast Nazi propaganda to English audiences.

Eventually common sense prevailed – the Home Service was to be 'lightened up' and programmes such as Tommy Hanley's ITMA (*It's That Man Again*) became an institution and loved by all except those who were being mocked even in a light-hearted manner. The 'posh' bosses of the country were worried that their Information Services were being compromised. The Liverpool lad Tommy had worked in music halls all over his local area and his humour was well understood in these places. They loved his fun which was usually directed at officialdom and those with posh accents. Then there was Arthur Askey – another Liverpool lad – along with Tommy Trinder, Flanagan and Allan, plus Anne Shelton and Vera Lynn. The comics also poked fun at the Germans and the singers avoided sad themes and concentrated on Victory ditties.

Radio was transmitted live in those days and this meant sticking to the script word for word in order to satisfy the censor. The 'secret' war did indeed also apply to radio. It was essential to play down bad news and to place extra emphasis on the occasional British successes during the early years of the conflict. The radio entertainers had to provide amusing or at least cheerful material. There were also occasions when the authorities altered the script in order to include coded instructions which could be picked up by agents in occupied Europe. In the days before television, the household 'companion' of the people was the radio and it is hard to realise today, with so much media choice available, the impact which the radio had. The idea of bringing *Workers' Playtime* into the factories, even though the locations were secret, was a master stroke.

The cinema was the 'going out' equivalent to the 'staying in' radio and the censor was also active in this area. The *Pathe News* items had to be 'suitably massaged' in order to foster optimism. At this time the cinema had a massive audience and 990 million paid for tickets to see films in 1940 and, by 1944, 1.5 billion tickets had been sold. Most people went to the cinema at least twice every week and each cinema changed its programme to reflect this demand. Folk like Margaret Hodges was 20 in 1939 and was a film fanatic all of her life,

I lived near Warrington and travelled all over the district collecting the names of picture houses including the Ritz, Odeon, Palladium. Palace, Tivoli, Roxy, Regal, Royal, Kings and many others, just like people collected car or train numbers. Some of the posher cinemas had their own

cafés but these have gradually closed down. Others had organs which rose from lifts in the floor and entertained the patrons during an interval when the 'A' film was to be followed by the news or the 'B' film, usually a comedy or a cartoon.

Popular films at the time had to be carefully vetted to please the censor. For example, *Mrs Miniver*, starring Greer Garson and Walter Pidgeon, which was released in 1942, depicts a lady with a stiff upper lip who would stand up to the German blitzes. In 1940 the Crown Film Unit was formed and made 29 short films during the war, the best of which was called *Target for Tonight*. This shows the heroes of a bomber 'giving it back' to the Germans. The film makers did not use actors but real airmen selected from bomber crews and it is sad to report that not one of those in the film survived the war.

Film companies at this time did have production problems. Their vast scenery and props warehouses had been requisitioned as part of the war effort and all raw materials were either in short supply or impossible to obtain. To make the film *Henry V* which depicts the battle of Agincourt in 1415 required the actors to wear chain mail. Margaret Hodges said to me,

Next time you watch this film, look out for the chain mail and have a laugh. I don't know how the studio did it but all of the armour was actually knitted.

Another thing which people remembered with regard to trips to the cinema was the very small clips which became known as 'food flashes'. These included 'How to weigh properly and save your rations'; 'Eat bread butter side down to improve the taste' and 'How to gut a herring'. There were also lots of recipes featured but how people were supposed to remember them or write them down in the dark is a mystery to me.

The theatres and the music halls were less popular than the pictures but this is not surprising. Apart from the fact that live performances were more expensive, there were very few of them in comparison to cinemas. Nevertheless, they had an important role to play during the war and the censor kept a close eye on the content. Shows like Ivor Novello's *Dancing Years* were popular during and after the war and performed by amateur as well as professional groups. These certainly played an important part in keeping up the spirits during the war and in the austere years which followed. Music hall acts popular in the North-West included George Formby, Frank Randle, Arthur Askey and Gladys Morgan, the Welsh comedienne whose high pitched laugh I can still remember to this day.

Apart from being entertained, many people during the war could find their own fun and dance halls were very popular. The success of the recent TV show, *Strictly Come Dancing*, proves that this form of enjoyment is far from dead. Initially in the war it was old-time and ballroom dancing which were popular but once the Americans arrived at places like Burtonwood, Warrington and Manchester, the jive and jitterbug became the rage. Some of the large dance halls were either taken over for the war effort or were just overwhelmed by the sheer numbers of enthusiasts. Every local church hall organised dances and some of the big stores such as Burtons the tailors opened up their vast storerooms to dancers. The Baths Hall in Victoria Road, Northwich, was a popular rendezvous and dances were held there most evenings, often sponsored by a wartime charity.

The sales of sheet music soared even though there was a shortage of paper. In houses with pianos and the venues used by local brass bands, the sound of *There'll Always Be An England*, *Roll Out the Barrel*, *Jerusalem*, and *Keep the Home Fires Burning* were known to one and all. Edward German's *Merrie England* was not initially popular because of his name but it was soon realised that he was British. Born in Shropshire in 1862, he died in 1936 and the song was a popular addition to the reservoir of music.

Apart from sheet music, records played on wind-up gramophones were part of almost every home and proved to be especially popular in the shelters. The records were very fragile and the metal needles were soon in short supply. Many children, myself included, were given the task of keeping the needles sharp by using a file. The popular artists of the time included Gene Autry the singing cowboy, Bing Crosby and Al Bowlly who was killed in the London Blitz. Then there was Gracie Fields, Anne Shelton and especially Vera Lynn. Here the records, which were not called discs in those days, were often purchased after having had a first airing on the radio.

Not only did entertainment keep up spirits during the war but when peace came there was an explosion of a different kind – this was the music of cheering! The celebrations firstly after the victory over Germany and then after the defeat of Japan led to massive euphoria. Union flags appeared as if by magic and where all the bunting came from is still a mystery to me. In the Burtonwood area, American flags provided an even more colourful mix. Church bells rang out, bonfires were lit and some fireworks suddenly appeared. One eight-year-old from Birkenhead heard these and shouted to his mother '*Has Hitler come back?*' There was singing, dancing, and all sorts of riotous behaviour; this went on day and night over a long period because nobody wanted to go home.

Megan Riley, whose two brothers had worked on mine-sweeping trawlers and who herself had worked in munition factories in Cheshire during the war, told me,

> *I remember celebrating both the VE and VJ days – I let so much hair down that I very nearly went bald!*

In Knutsford someone was touring the town winding a hand-cranked portable siren which was playing the continuous note of the 'All clear'. In Crewe and elsewhere all the locomotives with enough steam sounded their whistles and all around both banks of the Mersey, ships' sirens mingled with foghorns and church bells. One little group stood close to Birkenhead Priory and sang hymns including *Fight the Good Fight*. One song which certainly

Some of the sheet music that was popular during the war years
(above and right).

did not have a religious theme was *Hang Out the Washing on the Siegfried Line*, whilst a rival group tried to drown out the opposition with *There'll Always be an England*.

As street parties and bonfires appeared everywhere, a few workers had to be on red alert. Maud Johnson's grandfather worked at the Risley Ordnance Factory and she told me that,

> *He had to stay close to what he called the Big Bang Bunker and he was kept on firewatch and told to keep all the doors*

tightly shut as sparks from local bonfires sailed overhead in the wind.

Did this euphoria last? No, of course it didn't. Interspersed with boisterous parties held in streets and factories, the enjoyment was tempered with a real worry. Would full-time employment be a thing of the past and if rationing ceased, would prices go up to a point where some people could not afford to pay them? If truth be told, then the decade spanning 1945 and 1955 was even more worrying than at any time during the war. Winston Churchill lost

151

the 1945 election and the Labour leader Clem Atlee won with a massive majority. He was faced with an almost insurmountable economic problem.

The Beveridge Report aimed at a total reform of the social life of Britain and this was not before time. Indeed, before the war, Neville Chamberlain's government had hinted at progress along the same lines. Butler's Education Act came first which raised the school leaving age to sixteen and a tri-partite system of schools was developed consisting of grammar, technical and secondary modern schools. The pupils were selected by the use of a scholarship test and the measurement of IQs was the crude selection tool which was used. Jack Cunningham who was at teaching college with me, said,

I worked as a chemist for ICI during the war and many men and women who worked for me were brighter than I was and yet they had been forced to leave school at fifteen because their parents could not afford to let them stay on. Things improved after the Butler Act although there is still some way to go even in 2012.

From 1947 onwards, industries such as the mines and the railways were brought under government control whilst there was a new National Health Service, which was paid for by a National Insurance Scheme, and an improved unemployment scheme. There were, however, two major post-war problems. Firstly, there was an increase in unemployment especially in industrial areas which had concentrated upon armament, aerospace and shipbuilding. Cammell Laird, for instance, was no longer focussed upon the production of warships. There was, however, a demand to replace the lost merchant vessels and some of the ocean liners which had served as troop ships had to be refitted for the luxury market. Ben Fogarty remembers this time,

I was sixteen when the war ended and I started work at Lairds and I was really excited as I was working as an

apprentice joiner on the Mauritania. *She had been on active service for six years and she badly needed a refit. The timber we used was in short supply and I was helping to make staircases. We got into real trouble if we wasted even a couple of inches of timber. I remember how proud we all were when she sailed off to do her proper job but I still had a worry if there would be enough work in the yard to see me through my apprenticeship.*

Workers at the Crewe locomotive works had the same worry. John Spence was working at Crewe from 1939 to the early 1960s. He said,

After the war my worry was that we were the only country in Europe which was still reliant on steam. All of us were real railway men and knew that steam was literally running out but we made sure that our locomotives were the very best that we could produce. What devastated us was the suddenness of the decision to discontinue steam in the 1960s. We knew it was coming but it was the sheer speed which was the worry. Many people were put out of work at a stroke.

One problem which has never been fully addressed is the problem of rations which still applied in peacetime and went on after the restrictions were lifted. Many people thought that once the U-boat menace to the supply lines had disappeared, then imports would pour in straightaway. 'Dig for Victory' was not replaced by 'Dig for Peace'. What was not appreciated at the time was that overseas markets had also suffered in the war and they needed time to recover. In addition, the British merchant fleets had been devastated and the men and vessels from previously occupied countries, especially Norway, went home to address their own problems.

In view of this, it is not surprising that rationing continued until meat became freely available again in 1954. Sweets came off ration but demand meant that rationing had to be re-introduced. I remember travelling in a mucky old train to visit the Festival of Britain in London in 1951 and we had to change at Crewe. There was a man cleaning rust from a Nestlé's chocolate machine which had been out of use during the war years. The machine was painted red and when a three-penny piece was inserted, a thin bar of white chocolate was delivered. Newspapers, books and comics were in fierce competition with each other as decent quality paper became more freely available. The WH Smith unit was doing a roaring trade on the station and I bought a copy of *William and the Evacuees* by Richmal Compton.

The Festival of Britain itself was a great success and suggested a brighter future for all – a future that the people of Cheshire would help build.

Index

Other titles on Cheshire from Countryside Books

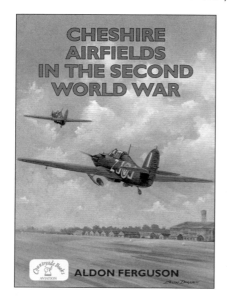

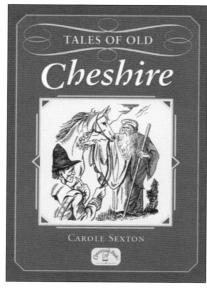